STAY THOU NEARBY

—— REFLECTIONS ON ——

THE 1978 REVELATION

ON THE PRIESTHOOD

**CAROL LAWRENCE-COSTLEY
AHMAD S. CORBITT
EDWARD DUBE
TRACY Y. BROWNING**

SALT LAKE CITY, UTAH

Author photographs © By Intellectual Reserve, Inc.

© 2023 Carol Lawrence-Costley, Ahmad S. Corbitt, Edward Dube, and Tracy Y. Browning,

All rights reserved. No part of this book may be reproduced in any form or by any means without permission in writing from the publisher, Deseret Book Company, at permissions@deseretbook.com. This work is not an official publication of The Church of Jesus Christ of Latter-day Saints. The views expressed herein are the responsibility of the authors and do not necessarily represent the position of the Church or of Deseret Book Company.

DESERET BOOK is a registered trademark of Deseret Book Company.

Visit us at deseretbook.com

Library of Congress Cataloging-in-Publication Data
CIP on file
ISBN 978-1-63993-181-1

Printed in the United States of America
University Press, Provo, UT

10 9 8 7 6 5 4 3 2 1

CONTENTS

Publisher's Preface 1

Directed by His Light 5
   Carol Lawrence-Costley

The Revelation That Changed the World 23
   Ahmad S. Corbitt

He Will Provide the Peace You Seek 49
   Edward Dube

Hope for a Better World 75
   Tracy Y. Browning

Notes 100

PUBLISHER'S PREFACE

In June 1978, a letter went out to members and leaders of The Church of Jesus Christ of Latter-day Saints throughout the world announcing that "the long-promised day has come." That day—that promise—extended to all worthy members of the Church all of the privileges and blessings of the priesthood and holy temple, without regard for race or color.

With that revelation, the era of priesthood and temple restriction based on race came to a close, but the questions and repercussions surrounding the policy reverberate still. The Church has provided an important resource with answers to many questions about the background, context, and aftermath of the priesthood revelation in its essay "Race and the Priesthood," available at topics.ChurchofJesusChrist.org. This collection of essays seeks to add to that body of knowledge by sharing reflections, insights, and experiences regarding the priesthood restriction from those for whom it is most personal—namely, from Black members of The Church of Jesus Christ of Latter-day Saints.

As we explore delicate questions regarding a policy that has led to pain, heartbreak, and even anguish, inevitably we will encounter a wide variety of individual reactions and responses. At the heart of so many disparate cries to the Lord for understanding and faith, however, we find the same yearning: "Stay Thou nearby." Whether in joy or pain, wherever we are in our journey toward understanding, no voice can bring peace to our souls like the Savior's. These essays from Church leaders who have navigated rough waters invite you to come and stay close to Christ, who offers healing and hope when none else can.

"I love when we are seen and heard. I truly believe that the more open we are when it comes to addressing hard topics for our members, the greater the healing. The priesthood ban was one of my crosses, and today I appreciate those open and willing to hear about and respect my journey, allowing me the space to share without discounting my experiences simply because they do not mirror their own journeys."

–CAROL LAWRENCE-COSTLEY

DIRECTED BY HIS LIGHT

―――――― ◇ ――――――

CAROL LAWRENCE-COSTLEY

Sister Carol Lawrence-Costley was born in London, England, to Mavis Gordon and Benjamin Lawrence. She received a master's degree from Brigham Young University in social work and currently works assisting individuals to overcome their addictions. Sister Lawrence-Costley is married to Jerry Costley. They have five children and six (soon to be seven) grandchildren. She has served in the Young Women and Relief Society in various capacities, as gospel doctrine teacher, activity days leader, Primary teacher, and Young Women camp director, and volunteered with a local theater and various social service organizations. She is currently a member of the Young Women General Advisory Council.

And when ye shall receive these things, I would exhort you that ye would ask God, the Eternal Father, in the name of Christ, if these things are not true; and if ye shall ask with a sincere heart, with real intent, having faith in Christ, he will manifest the truth of it unto you, by the power of the Holy Ghost.

And by the power of the Holy Ghost ye may know the truth of all things. (Moroni 10:4–5)

It was true, and I was ready to follow my Savior—officially. I wanted to let go of all my worldly ways and commit to The Church of Jesus Christ of Latter-day Saints. Even at fifteen, I understood that life came with challenges and that joining the Church would expose me to criticism from others because of my decision. After four years of investigating and waiting for my parents' consent, the approval finally came. The night before my special day, the missionaries visited me for a final interview. They wanted to make sure that I understood Church doctrine and that I was joining of my own volition.

The meeting began with a discussion about my understanding of the doctrine, and then the direction changed, and the conversation turned serious. My heart sank; I couldn't believe the words they were saying. The priesthood restriction rumors were true. How could this be? Why hadn't anyone told me?

My journey had begun as a preteen girl, living with my six siblings and parents, unaware of a life-changing event that had been waiting around the corner—a spiritual event that would impact every one of my life decisions from that point forward. The story of my conversion is important because it includes the impact of the priesthood ban on my life. Sorting through my own thoughts and feelings has helped me to understand my relationship with my Savior better and to rely on Him when life has become challenging. There have been times when I've had to hear Him for myself and not rely on the confusing and sometimes painful words of others, whether well-meaning or not.

I would not be a member of The Church of Jesus Christ of Latter-day Saints today if I had not been directed by His light. As a child, I discovered the power of the Spirit and its influence, which brought a little girl to the Savior. Eventually, other family members would join that little girl and strengthen her ever-growing testimony. Forty-eight years later, I better understand what Elder David A. Bednar meant when he taught that our conscience is a manifestation of the Light of Christ, enabling us to judge good from evil.[1] I recognized goodness, and that's how I knew the gospel was true.

> The Spirit of Christ is given to every man, that he may know good from evil; wherefore, I show unto you the way to judge; for everything which inviteth to do good, and to persuade to believe in Christ, is sent forth by the power and gift of Christ; wherefore ye may know with a perfect knowledge it is of God. (Moroni 7:16)

DISCOVERY OF THE LIGHT

On May 22, 1972, my family gathered around the TV to watch the Royal Variety Performance at the London Palladium—a yearly tradition for many households in England. We were always curious to see who would perform for our beloved queen. That year, the guests were the Osmond Brothers. I remember being mesmerized by the wholesome, energetic young men from America with long dark hair and huge smiles that exposed big white teeth. What about them drew me in? I didn't know. The next school day, they were the talk of the playground. Their popularity exploded after their performance. Soon, a popular teen magazine had a two-page spread of Donny drinking a McDonald's milkshake. His image was everywhere. My friends and I bought every magazine and newspaper article we could find. The more we read about the family, the more we wanted to know about them. Within a few weeks, we discovered they were religious and belonged to a church in which the members were called "Mormons," after a particular book of scripture they read. The adults in my life teased me as they witnessed my plunge into what they believed was teenage hysteria.

We were a group of impressionable preteen girls who, once we learned about the Osmonds' religion, latched on to the "Word of Wisdom" and began living it. We stopped drinking tea, and we vowed not to smoke, drink alcohol, use drugs, or engage in anything that would cause harm to our bodies. We also agreed to live by the strict moral standards of the Osmonds' church—including no intimate relationships until marriage. As we committed to living their religion, we scoured England to see if such a church existed in our area, and we found a ward in Croydon, Surrey.

My friend Vanessa spearheaded reaching out to the Church in Salt Lake, requesting that the missionaries come and teach us. In the meantime, we visited the local ward. They met in a social hall used for various functions, often including events that featured alcoholic beverages and cigarette smoking. Preparing for Sabbath-day worship was a chore. Still, despite those inconveniences, the atmosphere created by the speakers and the congregation, coupled with the presence of the Spirit, transformed the old meeting hall into a sanctuary. I remember attending what was termed a "fireside." I don't recall who spoke, but I remember what I felt. The only word I could use at the time to describe this experience was feeling *love*. The friendliness of those in attendance made me feel welcomed—like family. It was as though I were at home with long-lost friends. It all felt so familiar.

We were raised in a loving home with a mother and father who met the criteria of "goodly parents" (1 Nephi 1:1). They loved us and worked hard to provide us with a life that honored traditional values. They stressed the importance of education, good manners, faith in God, and charity toward others. Dad was service oriented and was often away helping others several nights each week. He was the go-to man among family, friends, and neighbors when they needed a handyman. My mum went to night school to learn secretarial skills and eventually became a nurse. My parents were Christian and sent us to church every Sunday for as long as I can remember. However, there was a different feeling among our *new* church friends. With my knowledge today, I attribute those "familiar but new" feelings to the Light of Christ. I did not know what to expect exactly, but I felt driven to attend The Church of Jesus Christ of Latter-day Saints, and it felt good! I understood that what I was experiencing was "the true Light, which lighteth every man that cometh into the world" (John 1:9). I felt a continuous prompting to continue attending and seeking.

The discovery of this light worked within me for many years. Caring adults, missionaries, and peers taught and nurtured me in the gospel. The village of people who surrounded me exposed me to a sweet spirit that brought peace and comfort to my life. I was a child. I had no inkling how this experience would change the rest of my life. An American missionary couple had a significant part in helping me transform, and I have often wished to remember their names. I am grateful to recall their faces along with images of time spent in their home for discussions and other activities. The women of the ward were vital. They shepherded the large influx of teenage girls attending weekly.

We finally heard back from Salt Lake that the missionaries were coming. Vanessa's nana was one of the few parents who embraced our enthusiasm for the Church, and she opened her flat and played hostess for the missionary event. Several of our friends came. There must have been at least fifteen girls and a couple of youth members from the Croydon Ward. We almost screamed with excitement when we heard the knock at the door. Two wide-eyed missionaries walked into that cozy home to find a room full of mostly girls wanting to know more about the Church. Now I understand how the sight of us might have overwhelmed them.

I spent the next four years as an investigator, attending church weekly and participating in activities. I remember holding a youth dance at my house. We had a huge greatroom where we pushed back the furniture and danced the evening away. My association with the Church was not always smooth sailing. One day while at school, one of my teachers pulled me aside to let me know that my newly found religion was not to be trusted, and she told me that the members were racist. It was so confusing, because that had been far from my experience. She told me stories about hatred, discrimination, and priesthood bans that seemed so far-fetched in my twelve-year-old mind. It was curious because the ward I attended had several Black families, and they were members. I challenged her beliefs and let her know she had it all wrong. No one had ever discussed these issues, so I let it go. I loved my new ward family. My teacher shook her head and shrugged her shoulders, disappointed in my refusal to believe what she was sharing. She never addressed the issue again.

One of my favorite experiences involved my best friend, Dee. Her parents were committed to their traditions and forbade her from attending church with the "Mormons." So, every Sunday, Dee and I would arrange a playdate. I would meet her halfway and hop on the bus to attend church. To this day, we still chuckle about our sneaky "playdates" to church. Can you imagine being upset over tween girls wanting to engage in wholesome activities at church? Dee's parents found out after two years, and that was the end of it. Despite the obstacles, at the age of twenty-one, Dee became a baptized member of the Church. I am happy to report that Dee is still an active member today.

FINDING MY PLACE

In 1975, the missionaries challenged my sister and me to get baptized. First, we had to get both of our parents' permissions. My father lived and worked in the United

States at the time, and his written permission had to come through the mail. It took about three months to get everything in order, but at last, the date of May 30, 1975, was selected for our baptisms. We were so excited! Finally, I would be an official member of The Church of Jesus Christ of Latter-day Saints. As was customary at the time, young women who pursued the Church due to the Osmonds were often interviewed to ensure that they were joining for the right reasons. It wasn't unusual to have two sets of missionaries present. On the night before our baptisms, there were more than two.

In hindsight, I realize the extra missionaries were there for reinforcement as they delivered the devastating news about the priesthood ban. By this time, the missionaries had visited our home for over three years, had eaten dinner with us, and yet had never addressed the issue of the priesthood. I was devastated. Suddenly, all the faces of my fellow Black Saints in the ward came to mind. *How could they be in a church that banned them from the priesthood?* With mounting confusion and hurt, I felt I couldn't do it—I could not join such a church. I had foolishly spent years arguing with my teachers, telling them that they had their facts wrong. I would tell them, "There is no prejudice. None." I had never experienced even a hint of discrimination or mistreatment from anyone. Many members were from different countries, several were Black, and everyone worked well together. Each week I basked in the feeling of love and unity. Why now?

The room fell silent, and I clarified that this news was a game changer. I couldn't do it. I could not be baptized.

Not now, not ever! My sister Jacqui's exclamation that she would be baptized broke a tension that had filled the room. While her comment broke the tension, my heart continued to hurt. The news made me feel disregarded as a person. Did God see me differently? Was I included in and considered a viable part of the great gospel plan?

Uncertain of my place, I struggled with the new and disappointing knowledge. It yanked the promise of an eternal family out of my reach. So, I would have no temple marriage or a husband with the priesthood to guide my family? What was the point if I could not access these tremendous blessings I had learned about over the years? Suddenly out of the corner of my eye, I saw the shyest of all the missionaries rise to his feet and bear a testimony that left all in the room quiet. He looked me in the eyes and said, "Carol, I promise you that by the time you are ready to be married, every worthy male member will have the priesthood." You could have heard a pin drop. That night I hung on to Elder Williamson's promise and agreed to be baptized. I had no idea that this young man had provided me with a revelatory experience. I was engulfed by a feeling of peace that I could not ignore. His promise made me feel that all would be well.

Fast forward three years. My family had moved to the United States. I was graduating from high school and heading off to Brigham Young University for the summer semester. The date was June 9, 1978. I was chatting on the phone with my dear friend, Dee, in England. Suddenly, my mother appeared in the kitchen with her arms flailing. "Carol, come quick!"

My impatient response was, "Mum, I can't. I am on a long-distance call to England."

Her voice and manner became more emphatic. She ignored my response and urgently said, "Your prophet is on the television. He is making a big announcement."

I asked Dee to hold, dropped the phone to the floor, rolled my eyes as teenagers often do, and hurriedly followed Mum into the living room. Then I heard it—President Spencer W. Kimball said that the priesthood would be extended to all worthy male members of the Church, without regard to race or color. It was almost unbelievable! But I knew it to be true because I felt it that night in 1975. Elder Williamson was right. I was eighteen, heading off to BYU, moving into adulthood, and approaching marrying age. Screams of joy erupted as the news sank in, and I shared it with Dee. I remember my sister did an interview on the radio, and members of my Westchester Ward rejoiced, especially dear Brother Gene Freedman, who had taken my older sister, Jacqui, under his wing since our arrival in the United States.

A deep sense of gratitude came over me for the efforts of President Kimball, who took the time to wrestle with the matter of the priesthood and bring it forth to the rest of the Brethren. Though initially wounded by the ban, my heart began to heal as I felt my Father in Heaven's love for me. I felt known and vital to the work. I could now enjoy the blessings of the temple just like everyone else. Fully invested, I rededicated my efforts to being a true disciple of Jesus Christ.

CROSSES TO BEAR

> Then said Jesus unto his disciples, If any man will come after me, let him deny himself, and take up his cross, and follow me. (Matthew 16:24)

The challenge presented by the priesthood ban was one of the many crosses I would bear—a refining process that would serve to help me hang on to truth even when my trials seemed insurmountable. Amidst the challenge, I consistently received comfort from a voice in my mind that breathed warmth into my heart. *It will all work out*, the voice said. When the missionaries confirmed the gift of the Holy Ghost, extra comfort came my way. My patriarchal blessing served as a source of strength to me as I heeded the warnings, recommendations, and blessings, as well as the promises contingent upon my faith and words of comfort tailored to my circumstances. As I deepened my commitment to the gospel, with the encouragement of my bishop, I decided to go to the temple and receive my endowment. As I did so, I came to understand the importance of my personal relationship with the Savior. My ability to hear Him was of the utmost importance. It allowed me to weather hurtful comments made by others that opened old wounds. It helped me to deflect harmful remarks and slights from others as they tried to express their understanding of the priesthood ban. Without fail, a familiar, calming voice reassured me that their explanations were incorrect. I am a daughter of God; He loves me and is acutely aware of my needs and the necessary journey

I must take to deepen my connection and commitment to the Savior.

I naively believed that extending the priesthood to every male in the Church would erase or abolish racism among members. I did not understand that the early pronouncements by prominent leaders were deeply rooted in the hearts and minds of some Church members. As I lived through my college years, I experienced the painful impact of these lingering beliefs. I was even more disappointed in later years when my children continued to face hurtful comments and statements in their seminary classes. I remember watching general conference in April of 2018 with my family in our home. It was during that time that it had become apparent that my children were struggling. We were so excited to see Sister Becky Craven, a member of our own ward, receive a calling as the Second Counselor in the Young Women General Presidency. The girls were delighted. They loved seeing a familiar face—I did too. As we watched the conference, my older daughter, whose overall demeanor suggested she was less than thrilled to be watching conference, noted that amid the group of Church leaders, other faces were missing. There was no one who "looked like her" in the general leadership of the Church. As I looked at the television, I saw the sea of homogeneous faces—a familiar sight to me as a forty-year-plus Church member. My words did not come. I had no answer to my daughter's questioning. There were times when I had wondered about that same question myself. As a teen and throughout my life, I recall combing through the pages of the *Ensign*, looking for images of members who were brown. They did not even have to be Black—just someone from a minority group—and it would make me smile and feel more connected as a member. Why was it so essential for me to see different faces—faces that were like mine? Why? Knowing where you come from is key, and knowing my own identity as a child of God was a journey. I had felt healing with the lift of the priesthood ban, but I still wanted more, and my girls did too. It was sad for me to see that they too longed for a feeling of belonging.

As I contemplated my daughter's questions, I felt the tears welling in my eyes, and I slipped away to my closet, where I said a quiet prayer. I prayed for my daughters, and I prayed that I would know what to tell them. My tears turned to sobs as I felt no answers were coming, and I was afraid that they would lose their testimonies of the gospel I cherished. I had many questions about race too; however, that reassuring voice had always saved me in so many ways. Living the gospel had made me a better person. It was my Liahona, and it served as a significant anchor in my life. That night I felt so alone. After speaking with my husband, Jerry, I went to bed thinking that maybe more changes would come. Without a doubt, by the time we reached 2020, there had been many changes. The Church magazines had pages peppered with people from around the world and from different minority groups, including people with disabilities. To me, that represented change, and I was pleased with it. We were getting better representation. But for my girls, it was not enough. They were still yearning.

All of us have hills to climb, hardships to face, questions that go unanswered, periods of uncertainty, and mundane moments interwoven with joy throughout our journeys to become disciples of Christ. Surrounding us is a village of people whose love and compassion lift us when our hands hang down. From my first introduction to the Church, I have always loved the connections we enjoy as brothers and sisters in our Church family. The feeling of belonging was key to my conversion, and it is now vital to my children as they continue their journeys. Within our Church community, we can be *lifted up* when we are down, receive service to fill a need, share when we have a surplus, and care for others whose hearts are failing. Also important is our need to feel safe, to have our concerns validated, and to be fully accepted.

For the last four and a half years, I have had the privilege of working with a group of amazing sisters of the Young Women General Presidency and their council members. These sisters have opened a window into a world of what it means to embrace our differences, to love, to serve, and to reach out to give support, comfort, and healing. All of these things helped to validate my feelings in such profound and meaningful ways. One of my favorite videos produced by the Relief Society, entitled "Just Like You," depicted the presidency and the council members sharing their crosses and conveying how alike we all are. The brief clip highlighted some of the common issues we face and attested to our unique journeys. I love when we are seen and heard. I truly believe that the more open we are when it comes to addressing hard topics for our members, the greater the healing. The priesthood ban was one of my crosses, and today I appreciate those open and willing to hear about and respect my journey, *allowing* me the space to share without discounting my experiences simply because they do not mirror their own journeys.

Although the ban ended in 1978, it did *not* end old ideas inside and outside the Church. In twelfth grade, I shared with a guidance counselor my desire to attend Brigham Young University. He hurriedly closed his office door, drew his chair close to mine, and began to offer what he thought would be "critical information" about BYU, including why he believed it would not be a good fit for me. I quickly and politely said, "Sir, before you say anything, you should know that I am a member of The Church of Jesus Christ of Latter-day Saints." He breathed an audible sigh of relief, but I still wonder to this day what he wanted to tell me. I guess it had something to do with the history and the lack of diversity at Brigham Young University in the late seventies.

POWER IN A COMMON PURPOSE

We are seeing progress within the Church. Our magazines, art, members, and leadership are beginning to reflect the diversity of our membership. The actions of leaders affirm the Church's position on the value of diversity and the infinite worth of all God's children. Providing an environment where all can realize their worth and relationship to God will help deepen the spiritual foundation we strive to create.

One of the challenges we face is that just as God gives

each of His children a measure of grace that matches the gifts, needs, and potential of each unique soul, so, too, should be the efforts among Church members toward their fellow Saints. Imagine if all of us gave others the space to work through their own salvation while maximizing their individual spiritual potential. What a joy it would be to receive fairness from others, and not to be left out because we do not fit a particular criterion. Inclusion is critical to our goal of creating an environment of unity. I believe that a sense of belonging is a *vital* human need. When members are in an environment where they feel valued by others, where others welcome and value their uniqueness, and where there are strong human connections, they will feel free to concentrate more fully on achieving their full spiritual potential. The events of the past will always be with us, but we can use them to better ourselves.

The Savior loves everyone; His invitation is inclusive. Unity in the gospel springs from the understanding that we are brothers and sisters in a genuine sense. As we strive to become like Christ, we will see all as He sees them and love as He loves them, and that love will fill us with a desire to see that no one is left out. Unity does not mean that we lose our individuality; it means that we respect and learn from our differences. When Paul spoke of unity, he compared the Church to a human body. Each part had different features and functions, but all were necessary—all components must work together for optimal functioning (see 1 Corinthians 12).

There is power in a common purpose. With openness and honesty, we can better grow from our history and archaic ideas. As we unite to sustain our leaders, deepen our commitment to living the gospel, and keep shared covenants, our love for Heavenly Father and Jesus Christ will unify us. "If ye are not one ye are not mine" (D&C 38:27). I have always had hope in the potential of The Church of Jesus Christ of Latter-day Saints to remove racism and hatred from our midst, because of His truth that we bear. We can overcome and be an example to the world. I have held this hope in my heart and believe we can achieve what others perceive as impossible. I sincerely appreciate the efforts to unite with others in our community and to build alliances with those in our community who are marginalized. I embrace President Nelson's petition when he said, "Today I call upon our members everywhere to lead out in abandoning attitudes and actions of prejudice. I plead with you to promote respect for all of God's children." He said that "God does not love one race more than another. His doctrine on this matter is clear. He invites *all* to come unto Him, 'black and white bond and free,' . . . your standing before God is not determined by the color of your skin."[2] Now I look forward to the day when we heed the words of our prophet and be an example of unity to the world.

"As I ministered to others, it became clear to me that the doctrine of Christ, especially faith in Jesus Christ and His Atonement, was the way to access the most potent source of divine power and peace for anyone struggling with anything related to the restored gospel or the Church that administers it."

—AHMAD S. CORBITT

THE REVELATION THAT CHANGED THE WORLD

―――― ◇ ――――

AHMAD S. CORBITT

Elder Ahmad S. Corbitt earned a degree in sociology and a law degree, both in New Jersey. He has worked as a trial lawyer, general counsel, and government and public relations executive in New Jersey, New York, and Delaware. Elder Corbitt has served as a full-time missionary in the Puerto Rico San Juan Mission, stake president in New Jersey, president of the Dominican Republic Santo Domingo East Mission, and First Counselor in the Young Men General Presidency. He is currently serving as a General Authority Seventy. He and his wife, Jayne, have six children and twelve grandchildren.

It was the end of tenth grade for me at John Bartram High School, a tough inner-city school in West Philadelphia with a student population that was about 90 percent Black. My siblings and I, like the other kids in our neighborhood, would enjoy a hot city summer. Water gushed from fire hydrants to cool off kids in cutoff shorts, and the sweltering heat rippled in waves from the softened asphalt of the black streets.

Our neighborhood was hot in other ways too. "Black

fever" ran high. It was 1978. These were the days of "Black power" and "Black pride." Slogans, music, and movies extolled the Blackness of our identities and heritage, pushing back on not only decades of discrimination against Black people but, more subtly, on the shame some Black people themselves felt about aspects of their own racial heritage. For our family, these feelings of heritage and the ability to not follow the crowd in the Black community were amplified by our interest in the Nation of Islam. We seemed odd to some who lived in ways we understood were self-destructive.

Crime, too, was heating up, as it did every summer. It was at once predictable and random in the City of Brotherly Love. And some of it was racial. When my Black friends and I walked home from school, it was not unusual for us to be chased by gangs of white youth with sticks and bricks and shouts of racial epithets as we passed through their all-white neighborhoods. We had similar problems with some Black youth as we passed through their areas or when they came into ours.

Dad had grown up in Harlem, and our family had faced challenges in the Philadelphia housing projects and row-home communities we lived in, so we had to be fairly street smart. But we were also taught to be appropriate and sensible. Mom always said our family had purpose. She kept a tight leash on us, not just to keep us alive but to help us succeed. To us, she seemed endowed with spiritual sensitivity. On one occasion, my older brother, Tony, wanted to go to a party just up the street on our block with his friend Eric, who lived across the street. Mom said "the Holy Ghost" told her she should not let him go. Of course, he became very upset. The denial did seem ridiculous given how close the party was and the fact he'd be with his friend. But she prevailed, and Tony angrily stayed in for the evening. The next day we were all shocked to hear Eric had been shot going home from the party. He was paralyzed from the waist down and died a few years later. Mom, whose credibility soared, had many similar experiences. She taught us to seek the guidance of God's Spirit and to follow His will.

Given this training, the spiritual experience I had that same summer seems fitting in hindsight, though it was something of a surprise at the time. I had been wondering if there really was a God. My desire to know Him and if He existed was intensifying. It was then that I had a vivid dream that remains one of the most significant and sacred of my life.[1]

It confirmed God's reality and set me on a path toward knowing Him. I felt so summoned by God through the dream that I arose early the next morning, a Sunday, determined to get closer to Him. I put on slacks and a dress shirt and walked to the nearest church.

The service was a Catholic mass in a traditional stone church, called Most Blessed Sacrament, two blocks away. Surprisingly, turnout was low and white. It seemed I was the only Black person there, joining longtime parishioners who now commuted from safer neighborhoods. I was also surprised by how comfortable I was with this racial dynamic. While many white individuals had had positive influence on my life, I had never worshipped with them.

Given the decidedly Black Nation of Islam and our later membership in the Black Protestant church in which I had been baptized, I'd simply never had the opportunity. Yet it seemed good. I distinctly remember shaking hands with an older working-class white man in a uniform during what my Catholic friends call the sign of peace.[2] I remember our mutual smiles. More importantly, I remember feeling that this cross-racial display of spiritual brotherhood was right, that it was pleasing to God.

QUESTIONS ASKED AND ANSWERED

During this same period, over 2,000 miles away in Salt Lake City, Utah, fifteen leaders of The Church of Jesus Christ of Latter-day Saints wrestled with a question that would significantly impact the Church, the world, and the entire human family on both sides of the veil. Although I had no idea who they were, they would profoundly change my life and my family—root and branch—as they considered their question: Should priesthood ordination be extended to all worthy male members (and thus temple blessings for all worthy members) of The Church of Jesus Christ of Latter-day Saints, including those of African descent, from whom it had been withheld? On June 8 of that year, President Spencer W. Kimball and his counselors in the First Presidency issued the answer in an official statement:

> Aware of the promises made by the prophets and presidents of the Church who have preceded us that at some time, in God's eternal plan, all

of our brethren who are worthy may receive the priesthood, and witnessing the faithfulness of those from whom the priesthood has been withheld, we have pleaded long and earnestly in behalf of these, our faithful brethren, spending many hours in the Upper Room of the Temple supplicating the Lord for divine guidance.

He has heard our prayers, and by revelation has confirmed that the long-promised day has come when every faithful, worthy man in the Church may receive the holy priesthood, with power to exercise its divine authority, and enjoy with his loved ones every blessing that flows therefrom, including the blessings of the temple. Accordingly, all worthy male members of the Church may be ordained to the priesthood without regard for race or color.[3]

Two years later, in 1980, my family moved from Philadelphia to southern New Jersey, where two full-time missionaries came to our home. We later learned they had fasted and prayed for direction and were led directly to our street and house. My mother felt to invite them in. We were taught by a series of missionaries, and both parents and all ten children were baptized over several years. So far, five of us have served full-time missions, including Mom after Dad passed away.[4] Three of the grandchildren have now served or are serving as full-time missionaries.

Looking back, I marvel at the minimal impact the former priesthood ban had on our decisions to join the Church. At a minimum, my mother and I knew about the ban, and some members and missionaries attempted explanations before we were baptized.[5] But even the ethos of that era, strongly reinforced in our family's racial experiences, did not inhibit us from accepting and embracing the restored gospel. Our spiritual and social experiences while learning about the Church, and the testimonies that grew out of these experiences, were such that I don't remember race being much of an issue. This was true even though our Latter-day Saint congregation was overwhelmingly white.

It was not until after I was baptized in 1980 that I seriously studied the former priesthood ban on people of African descent. That study took me on a journey that, thanks to the gospel of Jesus Christ, transcended race, ethnicity, and culture.

I think it is natural for many Black people who join or investigate The Church of Jesus Christ of Latter-day Saints to look into the priesthood ban. However, we should always remember that the center of our lives and therefore the focus of our study ought always to be Jesus Christ and His doctrine. No amount of study of the priesthood ban will save us from death and enable us to return to God to enjoy eternal life with our families. Only the doctrine of Christ can help us achieve these eternal goals. And, in my observation and experience, if we focus on the former to the neglect of the latter, we will stumble. As I sought to deepen my relationship with God, I found my focus and energy continually more centered on Jesus Christ and His Atonement. As I ministered to others, it became clear to me that the doctrine of Christ, especially faith in Jesus

Christ and His Atonement, was the way to access the most potent source of divine power and peace for anyone struggling with anything related to the restored gospel or the Church that administers it.[6]

The Prophet Joseph Smith's declaration about "the testimony of Jesus" sprang to new life for me (Revelation 19:10; see also Doctrine and Covenants 76:51). "The fundamental principles of our religion," he said, "are the testimony of the Apostles and Prophets, concerning Jesus Christ, that He died, was buried, and rose again the third day, and ascended into heaven; and all other things which pertain to our religion are only appendages to it."[7]

As my focus on Christ and His Atonement increased, the vision of Heavenly Father's unified human family became clearer. Correspondingly, the priesthood ban and its particulars diminished in importance for me personally. I have also seen this with other Latter-day Saints who struggled with the former ban. They became converted to the restored gospel of Jesus Christ—and remained in His Church—only as they gained a personal witness and understanding of the doctrine of Christ and applied it in their lives.

The doctrine of Christ includes faith in Jesus Christ and His Atonement, repentance, baptism into The Church of Jesus Christ of Latter-day Saints, receiving the gift of the Holy Ghost, and enduring to the end. In my case, understanding Jesus's Atonement changed my self-perception forever. It catapulted my identity as a child of God, a child of the covenant, a disciple of Christ, a minister of the gospel, and a brother in the human family far above even the most socially ingrained aspects of my Black identity, despite my intense racial experiences. I believe one of the ways it accomplished this was, ironically, by giving me a sense of my own nothingness without Christ. Suddenly, the principles, teachings, and experiences of prophets in the scriptures, especially the Book of Mormon and Pearl of Great Price, awakened a vision of my utter dependence upon Jesus and my dire need of His salvation and to follow Him. Far from having a problem with His Church, I saw more keenly than ever how supremely blessed I was to be a part of it and what a profound honor it was to help establish it as much as I could. This deep spiritual self-perception didn't diminish my earthly racial identity at all. On the contrary, it contextualized and magnified it in eternity.[8]

CHRIST'S PROMISED BLESSINGS

This experience and perspective helped me see that all humanity shared a common desperate need for a Savior and that there was, therefore, no appreciable difference between any of us from prince to pauper. None of us could receive salvation or eternal life without Jesus Christ and His Atonement, and therefore everything else was vanity. If it detracted from our focus on Him or distracted us from coming unto Him, it was a hindrance, and of the worst kind. All of this enabled me to understand race and ethnicity from a more eternal perspective,[9] to more clearly see persons of all races and ethnicities as my true brothers and sisters and to truly love them all as Christ does.

I believe that as our understanding of these principles increases, another breathtaking reality comes into focus, like a familiar scripture passage that suddenly leaps off the page with new meaning and power. We see that The Church of Jesus Christ of Latter-day Saints is uniquely able and divinely destined to become the most unifying global organization in the history of the world. We all need to help each other focus on Jesus Christ and apply His doctrine as He has invited and avoid distractions and relying on our own wisdom or the world's philosophies and ideologies. Clearly, the Savior's Church and the gospel it administers transcend race, ethnicity, and culture. The Church exists largely to gather and unify the Father's children from every nation on the earth as brothers and sisters. At a general conference of the Church with members from all over the world, President Henry B. Eyring taught:

> My beloved brothers and sisters, it is a joy to be gathered with you. . . . We live in many different circumstances. We will come from every nation and many ethnic backgrounds into the kingdom of God. And that prophesied gathering will accelerate. . . .
>
> . . . My message of hope today is that a great day of unity is coming. The Lord Jehovah will return to live with those who have become His people and will find them united, of one heart, unified with Him and with our Heavenly Father.[10]

President Eyring emphasized that having our "hearts changed through the Atonement of Jesus Christ . . . is the only way God can grant the blessing of being of one heart."

My experience bears witness that this is true. Given the Church's powerful potential and prophesied future in unifying God's children, what do I say when asked about the priesthood ban? How do I urge Church members to respond if they are asked, "Is the Mormon Church racist?" or, "How can you belong to a church that once discriminated against Black people?" When I was serving as stake president, a sincere, newly baptized Black couple asked me to help them respond to these questions.

Rather than look backward and attempt to provide a historical explanation, I felt impressed to help this couple look forward toward God's revealed vision for His children—an approach I believe is essential for all people. Elder Jeffrey R. Holland taught, "Faith is always pointed toward the future."[11] If we don't learn how to look forward with an eye of faith, as the Book of Mormon teaches,[12] I believe we will never develop sufficient faith in Christ to realize and receive His promised blessings of unity and harmony. I told my friends that The Church of Jesus Christ of Latter-day Saints is one of the most successful international organizations in the world at promoting brotherhood and sisterhood among all races and ethnicities, including people of African descent.[13] They were surprised. I explained that our Church is uniquely empowered and destined to achieve worldwide peace, harmony, and unity among all willing peoples of the earth.

How has the Lord positioned and empowered The Church of Jesus Christ of Latter-day Saints to achieve such a vast and wonderful mission—to bring unity to the human family? To answer the question, we must remember that through His Atonement, Jesus Christ transforms the way we view ourselves and the entire human family. He transforms the way we see the Church, its leaders, its gathering and saving mission, its members, and the restored gospel in general. No ideology, philosophy, or methodology can accomplish this. When Jesus promised peace, He said, "Not as the world giveth, give I unto you" (John 14:27). I understand Him to mean the world will never be able to give the peace that only He can give. I believe the same is true of unity. *Unity I leave with you. My unity I give unto you; my racial harmony, my oneness as a people I give unto you, but not as the world giveth, give I unto you.* Those who have felt the sting of racism and prejudice in their lives, as I have, understandably may fear that trusting in the Lord and His ways may not work. Perhaps this is why Jesus then stated: "Let not your heart be troubled, neither let it be afraid." His kingdom is not of this world, He has many times taught. Therefore, we should not expect that this world's methods or philosophies will accomplish His purposes.

ONGOING REVELATION

I have also found Moroni's counsel especially powerful and instructive for how the Lord would have us think about what President Dallin H. Oaks aptly called "disappointments of the past."[14] Seeing latter-day humanity, Moroni stated, "Behold, I speak unto you as though I spake from the dead; for I know that ye shall have my words." He then shared this important principle that is easily missed but is so relevant for us today: "Condemn me not because of mine imperfection, neither my father, because of his imperfection, neither them who have written before him; but rather give thanks unto God that he hath made manifest unto you our imperfections, that ye may learn to be more wise than we have been" (Mormon 9:30–31). Because everyone and everything in our fallen world is imperfect, and since there's "an opposition in all things" (2 Nephi 2:11), there will likely be both negative and positive in any given circumstance. I hear Mormon teaching that recognizing imperfection, even in sacred things, is not bad when we do so humbly in order to become wiser than those who preceded us. But when we condemn or judge others for their imperfections, we put ourselves in real peril. This jeopardy takes many forms, including distraction from our own sins, imperfections, and need to repent; inability to exercise strong faith in Christ; lack of gratitude with a myopic focus on ourselves or our personal interests; and missing the big picture of the Lord's grander purposes. Mormon warned latter-day humanity about the last—specifically missing the Book of Mormon's great purposes in the Lord's eternal plan. But this vital principle applies to harshly judging or condemning any of the Lord's workers, imperfect though they may be, and not seeing them as He does.

As President Brigham Young taught, "This work is a progressive work, this doctrine that is taught the Latter-day Saints in its nature is exalting, increasing, expanding and extending broader and broader until we can know as we are known, see as we are seen."[15] When we truly live the doctrine of Christ, as we keep our covenants with

God and serve His children, we no longer look at each other and the world, in Paul's words, as if "through a glass darkly" (1 Corinthians 13:12). Instead, we begin to know and see ourselves and others as God knows and sees all His children. This godly viewpoint helps us perceive that ancient and modern prophecies are being fulfilled: God is "gather[ing] together in one all things in Christ" (Ephesians 1:10). This divine perspective and the Book of Mormon principle of not condemning also help us avoid the serious burden of making ourselves the judges of God's servants from the past, who likely have repented and been forgiven by Jesus Christ. This may be one reason why the Savior proclaimed, "I, the Lord, will forgive whom I will forgive, but of you it is required to forgive all men" (D&C 64:10).

When I studied the former priesthood ban, over time I came to understand that the Lord had always intended His Church to grow beyond its initial organization. It was equally clear that this could happen only under the direction of living prophets and apostles.[16] The Lord commanded Joseph Smith, "a seer, a translator, a prophet, an apostle of Jesus Christ," to "lay the foundation [of the Church], and to build it up unto the most holy faith" (D&C 21:1–2). Like its members, God's restored Church, it seemed, was to undergo a process—"line upon line, precept upon precept, here a little and there a little" (2 Nephi 28:30)—before it could become the fully constituted, universally unified, global body of Saints He intended.[17] The Lord has declared that as we "give heed unto all [the prophet's] words and commandments which he shall give unto [us] as he receiveth them . . . the Lord God will disperse the powers of darkness from before [us]" (D&C 21:4–6). I believe the 1978 revelation on the priesthood—"a new flood of intelligence and light"[18] received by prophets and apostles—was one of the most powerful beams of heavenly light in the history of the world. I'm convinced it led to a major phase in the Lord's efforts to build up His Church "unto the most holy faith" (D&C 21:2) and unify His children in all nations.

It's impressive to me that a revelation of this magnitude, one of the most universally known revelations received in the modern era (perhaps better known outside the Church than even Joseph Smith's First Vision), relates positively to people of African descent and to the ministry of apostles and prophets. How did this historic revelation extending the priesthood to all worthy males come about? What follows is a brief overview of how the revelation itself was received.

On one occasion, after numerous petitions to God to extend the priesthood to all worthy males, the First Presidency and the Quorum of the Twelve, led by President Spencer W. Kimball, counseled together about whether to repeat the petition. They stated they were eager for their Black brothers and sisters to receive all the blessings of the restored gospel.[19] President Kimball invited his counselors in the First Presidency and each member of the Quorum of the Twelve to share their personal opinions on this vital question.[20] President Thomas S. Monson, who served as President of the Church for almost ten years, and who was the last surviving participant in the revelation, took part in that meeting. He echoed the desire of others when he said that he "favored petitioning the Lord again with the plea to extend the priesthood to all men counted worthy."[21]

President Gordon B. Hinckley told of the revelation he and his brethren received in response to their petition. "All of us knew that the time had come for a change and that the decision had come from the heavens," he said. "The answer was clear. There was perfect unity among us in our experience and in our understanding."[22] President Boyd K. Packer's biographer wrote, "Those of the Lord's watchmen who were present at those historic times will recall and have borne witness to the Spirit of revelation that attended them, and each has expressed gratitude for being part of the momentous experience."[23] With love, unity, and devotion to the Lord, these brethren reversed a ban that had already been longstanding by the time each had been born.[24]

I feel that our loving Eternal Father, mindful of His earthly Black children, poured out a powerful spirit of unity from the heavens that would eventually fill the whole earth. Through apostles and prophets, He once again hastened His work in its time,[25] summoning the entire human family—all races and ethnicities—to an increased "unity of the faith" and a more complete spiritual brotherhood and sisterhood.

Although more than four decades have passed since the revelation on the priesthood, some continue to have questions about the priesthood ban. And while enemies of the Church will likely always try to leverage it for their own designs, in my experience, some who ask these questions sit in our seminary, institute, and Sunday classes and before our full-time missionaries. Their motivation in asking questions is usually sincere and heartfelt, born of spirit-deep feelings of justice, fairness, and love. They are not unlike some of Jesus Christ's ancient disciples who once asked questions about a man who suffered a disability from birth. "Master, who did sin, this man, or his parents, that he was born blind?" Jesus's disciples queried. Recognizing God to be just, they thought the denial of such a basic blessing as sight must have been a punishment for someone's sinfulness—either the man's own, in the premortal world, or his parents', sometime before he was born. Jesus's answer taught a powerful lesson that I believe relates to the priesthood ban: "Neither hath this man sinned, nor his parents: but that the works of God should be made manifest in him" (John 9:2–3).

I hear the Savior's answer this way: *You're not asking the right question or thinking from a godly perspective.*[26] *You're trying to make sense of a sad situation by assigning blame without knowing all the facts; but I see this man's condition as an opportunity for me to bless him and show forth the power of God through a miraculous work.*

How does this story relate to the priesthood ban? I believe when we analyze the priesthood ban in a way that seeks to assign blame, either to early leaders of the Church or to people of African descent—and blame has been assigned to both groups—we become distracted. According to Jesus's teaching, we have a beam in our eye that blinds us from seeing clearly. We miss the Lord's grander, more eternal vision and opportunity. We essentially ask,

"Master, who did sin, Black people or the early Church leaders, that the priesthood ban was imposed?" I believe if the Savior stood beside us, His answer would be just as forward-looking and glorious as His response to His disciples' question about the blind man: *Neither have my Black children sinned, nor the prophets: but that the power of God should be made manifest through a miraculous work.*[27]

THE WORKS AND POWER OF GOD MADE MANIFEST

How are the works and power of God made manifest in relation to the priesthood ban? My experience suggests that because the prior ban is still well known, many people may not expect The Church of Jesus Christ of Latter-day Saints to achieve a worldwide multiracial brotherhood and sisterhood. But this is precisely what the Church has done, is doing, and is destined to do.[28] President Henry B. Eyring taught that "a great day of unity is coming" at a time "in which we will be prepared as a people for our glorious destiny."[29]

I believe the Church's present and continuing success in achieving unity across the earth will "attract the gaze of all the world in latter days."[30] The world will be amazed by this accomplishment. Many will come to recognize this achievement not as the mere work of clever men and women but as part of the prophesied "marvellous work and a wonder" (Isaiah 29:14) and "great day of unity" God Himself is bringing to pass for the salvation of His children in the last days through the restored gospel of Jesus Christ.[31] As President Ezra Taft Benson long ago taught,

"Only the gospel will unite men of all races and nationalities in peace. Only the gospel will bring joy, happiness, and salvation to the human family."[32] President Howard W. Hunter taught, "It is in understanding and accepting [the] universal fatherhood of God that all human beings can best appreciate God's concern for them *and their relationship to each other*. This is a message of life and love that strikes squarely against all stifling traditions based on race, language, economic or political standing, educational rank, or cultural background."[33] He stated, "Race makes no difference; color makes no difference; nationality makes no difference. The brotherhood of man is literal. We are all of one blood and the literal spirit offspring of our eternal Heavenly Father . . . [and] literal brothers and sisters as well. This is a fundamental teaching of The Church of Jesus Christ of Latter-day Saints."[34] Under the leadership of President Spencer W. Kimball, the First Presidency stated, "Our message . . . is one of special love and concern for the eternal welfare of all men and women, regardless of religious belief, race, or nationality, knowing that we are truly brothers and sisters because we are sons and daughters of the same Eternal Father."[35]

More recently, members of the First Presidency reaffirmed this teaching. President Russell M. Nelson has taught, "The gospel of Jesus Christ is exactly what is needed in this confused, contentious, and weary world . . . no other message can eliminate contention in our society."[36] Similarly, President Dallin H. Oaks stated, "Only the gospel of Jesus Christ can unite and bring peace to people of all races and nationalities."[37] And it is never too late. President Henry B. Eyring stated, "God has promised that blessing [of unity] to His faithful Saints whatever their differences in background and whatever conflict rages around them."[38]

Let us allow the differences we see among God's children in the Church and throughout the world remind us of our important role in helping unify everyone "in perfect peace and harmony." There is a clear sense that we as a people are doing so much better. President Dieter F. Uchtdorf affirmed, "This is truly a universal Church, with members spread across the nations of the earth proclaiming the universal message of the gospel of Jesus Christ to all, irrespective of language, race, or ethnic roots."[39] The Lord declared, "The righteous shall be gathered out from among all nations, and shall come to Zion, singing with songs of everlasting joy" (D&C 45:71). We are seeing this, our Heavenly Father's vision, unfold before our eyes. All people of every race, ethnicity, and culture—all nations, kindreds, tongues, and people—are coming together "in perfect peace and harmony."[40] The Church of Jesus Christ of Latter-day Saints is ordained and destined to fulfill this glorious, supernal vision. The Lord's servants invite each of us to be part of it!

Leaders of The Church of Jesus Christ of Latter-day Saints especially call upon members of our Church—whether adults or youth—who engage in attitudes or actions of racism to repent of this sin. As declared in the official Church statement issued on February 29, 2012, "The Church's position is clear— . . . We do not tolerate racism in any form . . . including any and all past racism by individuals both inside and outside the Church."[41] While this statement is not an indictment of the whole Church or its members, generally, President Gordon B. Hinckley's lamentation of 2006 sadly applies to some today: "Racial strife still lifts its ugly head. I am advised that even right here among us there is some of this. I cannot understand how it can be." He added, "Now I am told that racial slurs and denigrating remarks are sometimes heard among us. I remind you that no man [or woman or child] who makes disparaging remarks concerning those of another race can consider himself a true disciple of Christ."[42]

In the June 1, 2018, Be One celebration commemorating the revelation on the priesthood, President Oaks stated, "As we look to the future, one of the most important effects of the revelation on the priesthood is its divine call to abandon attitudes of prejudice against any group of God's children. Racism is probably the most familiar source of prejudice today, and we are all called to repent of that." He continued his strong admonition, "As servants of God who have the knowledge and responsibilities of His great plan of salvation, we should *hasten* to prepare our attitudes and our actions—institutionally and personally—to abandon all personal prejudices."[43] At subsequent general conference and Brigham Young University addresses, President Oaks reaffirmed these teachings and his call to "root out racism" from among us.[44]

President Russell M. Nelson has taught, "Each of us has a divine potential because each is a child of God. Each is equal in His eyes. The implications of this truth are profound. Brothers and sisters, please listen carefully to what

THE REVELATION THAT CHANGED THE WORLD

I am about to say. God does not love one race more than another. His doctrine on this matter is clear. He invites *all* to come unto Him, 'black and white, bond and free, male and female.' I assure you that your standing before God is not determined by the color of your skin. Favor or disfavor with God is dependent upon your devotion to God and His commandments and not the color of your skin."[45] He "call[ed] upon our members everywhere to lead out in abandoning attitudes and actions of prejudice."[46] With their unifying keys that "bring the children of Adam and Eve to a unity of the faith in Jesus Christ,"[47] they are calling the human family together and teaching us how to be unified in Christ and to "live together in love" (D&C 42:45).

I believe The Church of Jesus Christ of Latter-day Saints will increasingly shine and stand apart in unity, in contrast to the racial and ethnic tensions and clashes throughout the world. Note President Eyring's further insight: "We see increased conflict between peoples in the world around us. Those divisions and differences could infect us. . . . The need for that gift [of unity] to be granted to us and the challenge to maintain it will grow greater in the days ahead."[48] We are infected by divisions and challenged to maintain unity when we allow ourselves to be deceived by the world's ideologies such as racist attitudes, words, and actions. We are also infected when we go about changing such attitudes in ways that are worldly, contentious, or otherwise not Christlike. Academic, governmental, and other cultural approaches may coerce behavior, but they won't change hearts, which is why the prophets have taught that only the gospel can enable the unity we seek. President Eyring promised that despite challenges to unity, the "prophesied gathering will accelerate."[49] Regardless of how the priesthood ban came about, I'm convinced our Heavenly Father is forwardly focused on using it to show the world His works and His power to unify His earthly children of all colors in peace and love.[50] I feel He wants each of us to have this same higher, forward-looking focus.[51]

We move toward this higher focus as we learn about the true nature of God and our relationship to Him—truths revealed through latter-day apostles and prophets. Brotherhood and sisterhood through the gospel of Jesus Christ, irrespective of race, ethnicity, and culture, has always been a central message of The Church of Jesus Christ of Latter-day Saints. In "The Family: A Proclamation to the World," the First Presidency and Quorum of the Twelve Apostles state: "All human beings—male and female—are created in the image of God. Each is a beloved spirit son or daughter of heavenly parents, and, as such, each has a divine nature and destiny. . . . In the premortal realm, spirit sons and daughters knew and worshipped God as their Eternal Father."[52] As President Russell M. Nelson has taught, "Only the comprehension of the true Fatherhood of God can bring full appreciation of the true brotherhood of man. That understanding inspires passionate desire to build bridges of cooperation instead of walls of segregation."[53]

It stands to reason that Satan would want to instigate distrust of the apostles and prophets. If he can divert the

Saints from following them, he can lead them off of the covenant path and keep God's children divided. He surely has many methods for doing this, but inciting activism toward the Church seems the most effective with the Lord's valiant Saints. This approach deceives Church members into seeing themselves as holding apostles and prophets "accountable" and directing worldly tactics of secular activism against the Lord's own Church and its leaders. This obviously sets them up as critics of these leaders and subtly pits them against the Lord's anointed. However, it deceptively does so in a way that tricks such members into feeling noble and part of a righteous cause.[54]

In my early youth, as I learned about prophets, seers, and revelators and accepted them as living prophets, I never could have anticipated that I would one day receive a telephone call from one of them and actually discuss the revelation with him. But while I was working on an earlier version of this very essay in June 2012—thirty-four years to the month after the revelation—my cell phone rang.

"Brother Corbitt?" the distinguished voice asked.

"Yes, this is Ahmad Corbitt."

"Elder Perry!" the voice replied.

Not accustomed to receiving such direct phone calls, I responded, "Elder L. Tom Perry?" probably sounding ridiculous.

"That's right!" he answered, ignoring my clumsiness.

He shared the purpose of his call, which related to my Church assignment in New York at the time. He had no idea about the essay I was writing. I thought it remarkable—a true tender mercy—that the only phone call I've ever received directly from one of the Apostles who participated in the revelation on the priesthood came at the precise time I was writing about this topic, and in the same month as the revelation. The following is an excerpt from my journal entry about that conversation, which Elder Perry gave me permission to share:

> At some point, I told Elder Perry that I was writing about the topic of the priesthood and African peoples. At that moment it occurred to me for the first time (so far as I can recall) that Elder Perry participated in the priesthood revelation. . . . Elder Perry . . . shared with me that the priesthood revelation experience was for him the most spiritual and significant experience in the Brethren's Thursday Temple meetings in his thirty-eight years of attending them! He said the same was true for all the Senior Brethren at the time. His special witness touched me by the power of the Holy Ghost. I began to become emotional and asked him to excuse my emotion. In a subdued voice, he then added, "We were not alone."

The Lord restored the priesthood and laid the foundation of the Church, thus restoring the fullness of the gospel of Jesus Christ to the world. The ancient apostolic keys that were angelically bestowed upon Joseph Smith have been transferred in their entirety upon all of the Presidents of the Church, and they rest today upon our living Prophet. I marvel and wonder at the Father's work in these last days as He miraculously gathers His sons and daughters of all races and ethnicities into a common covenant family through the restored gospel.

I know the First Presidency and the Quorum of the Twelve Apostles received a revelation from the Lord in June of 1978. At the time, I felt it without understanding it. I witness that through those latter-day apostles and prophets, God parted the heavens and opened an effectual door for all His children to receive a fullness of His blessings. In my view, those leaders were instruments in the Lord's hands to bring about one of the most significant worldwide changes necessary to prepare God's children for the Second Coming of Jesus Christ. "Change the world" is a popular phrase, but the priesthood revelation truly has changed the world! All the recipients of that revelation have passed on to the spirit world. I'm convinced they now know the revelation they received changed that world too.

"A peace gradually enveloped my thoughts. The discouragement, sadness, and devastation I had felt earlier that evening were lifted. I felt a sense of quiet contentment enfolding me. I felt warm inside. This warmth continued to spread throughout my body. All I could think was how tender and sweet this feeling was, of knowing that my answer to my question lay in what happened in 1820."

–EDWARD DUBE

HE WILL PROVIDE
THE PEACE YOU SEEK

◇

EDWARD DUBE

Elder Edward Dube was born in Chirumhanzu, Zimbabwe, on May 12, 1962. He was sustained as a General Authority Seventy of The Church of Jesus Christ of Latter-day Saints on April 6, 2013. At the time of his call, he had been serving as a member of the Third Quorum of the Seventy in the Africa Southeast Area. He is currently serving as the President in the Africa South Area Presidency.

Elder Dube received a diploma in education in 1992 from Zimbabwe D.E. College and studied entrepreneurship at the University of South Africa. He has worked in many positions for the Church Educational System in Africa and served in several Church callings, including full-time missionary in Zimbabwe, district president, branch president, stake president, president of the Zimbabwe Harare Mission, and Area Seventy. Elder Dube married Naume Keresia Salizani on December 9, 1989. They are the parents of four children.

The overarching reason many Black African leaders and members came to understand and find peace about the revelation on the priesthood in June 1978, and the prohibition on the priesthood for those of African descent until that time, is their testimony of the gospel. Many discovered this prohibition after they had a testimony of

Heavenly Father and Jesus Christ's appearance to the boy Joseph Smith in the spring of 1820, and a testimony of the Book of Mormon. And that has been my experience, too.

My faith journey as it relates to this topic began while I was on my mission.

The first time I heard about the prohibition on the priesthood for those of Black African descent was on my mission. I was baptized in 1984 after the prohibition had already ended. Two years later, I was called to serve in the South Africa Johannesburg Mission.

While assigned to Bulawayo, Zimbabwe, my companion Elder Francis Jack and I visited a less-active sister. Her husband was a theological professor from another church. He asked us why the priesthood had been withheld from men of Black African descent. He said many things that bothered me—things I had never heard before. Among the things he mentioned were that Church leaders had claimed that this prohibition came from God. He also gave unfounded explanations, including a curse on Cain and his descendants. My companion and I sat quietly, dumbfounded by the eloquence of this man, who concluded by reading Official Declaration 2 from the Doctrine and Covenants, which I hadn't even known existed. He discussed the politics that were happening around the world, with most African countries gaining independence, and claimed that the Church leaders had yielded to pressure in claiming that the revelation was from God.

When I walked out of that home, I felt very low, very discouraged, and devastated. Elder Jack and I rode our bikes back to our apartment without speaking to each other that evening. This was a good 10-kilometer (6.2-mile) ride, from the Famona suburb to the city center where we lived. In my mind, I found this prohibition very unfair. The man's words were distressing. I felt agony, anguish, and torment. I felt torn apart. I knew the gospel was true and loved what I was doing as a missionary of The Church of Jesus Christ of Latter-day Saints. Yet this discovery of the priesthood prohibition was stabbing my heart. I just could not get through my shock at this news. My mind was full of turmoil, repeating the words, *It was so wrong and so unfair.*

When we arrived at our apartment, my junior companion Francis Jack, also a Black African missionary, looked at me and said, "Elder Dube, what is wrong with you? You seem very disturbed. Are you all right?"

"Didn't you hear what he said?" I responded. "How could this happen?"

"Elder, do you believe that Heavenly Father and Jesus Christ appeared to the boy Joseph?"

"Yes," I said. "But what does that have to do with this?"

"It has everything to do with it," Elder Jack replied. "We believe in revelation, don't we?"

As we were ready to retire to bed, Elder Jack sensed my mood, and although it was my turn to offer the nightly prayer, he volunteered to pray. During his prayer, after our normal prayer for the people in our teaching pool, he asked Heavenly Father to pour out His Spirit so that we could overcome the influence of the adversary who comes in different forms. Then he prayed specifically for me that my "faith fail not" and that I should focus on our purpose as missionaries (see Luke 22:32). Although I protested after the prayer that my concern had nothing to do with my faith, I took time to reflect on my companion's pleading for my faith to be strengthened. I thought about his words and what the professor had said. I thought about what had happened in the spring of 1820. I asked myself this question: *Did Heavenly Father and Jesus Christ appear to Joseph Smith?* The impressions I had felt over and over while teaching were overwhelming. Yes, They did appear. Why was there a prohibition on the priesthood for those of Black African descent? I reflected upon the scripture I had committed to memory: "Surely the Lord God will do nothing, but he revealeth his secret unto his servants the prophets" (Amos 3:7). Following the footnotes, I read Ammon's teachings to the people of Limhi: "But a seer can know of things which are past, and also of things which are to come, and by them shall all things be revealed, or, rather, shall secret things be made manifest, and hidden things shall come to light, and things which are not known shall be made known by them . . . which otherwise could not be known" (Mosiah 8:17). When I read this verse in the Book of Mormon, I realized with surprise that a feeling of serenity had replaced the troubling thoughts I had endured a couple of hours prior. Although I began fumbling through that scripture with hostility, I had to admit that something was captivating about this discovery of how the Lord reveals His secrets to the ancient and modern prophets.

I felt that this prohibition on the priesthood for those

of Black African descent had none of the excessively sentimental expressions to which the professor had alluded. In such an era of great racial division in the United States, where many people of African descent lived in slavery and with racial distinctions and prejudice, I sensed the predicament that the leaders were faced with. I no longer sensed a foreboding about what I had heard earlier. Nor were there any worrying impressions hovering over my thoughts about this subject. It all seemed so refreshing. With that experience, I slowly drifted into a deep sleep.

THE SPIRIT OF PEACE

A few hours later, I woke up in the middle of the night. I felt happy and at peace.

The answer to every gospel question ties back to what happened in 1820. Knowing that Heavenly Father and Jesus Christ appeared to Joseph Smith means knowing that he was a prophet and that this is the Lord's Church. If Heavenly Father and Jesus Christ appeared to the boy Joseph, then all gospel principles and questions fall into place. This is a church of revelation, and the Lord reveals certain processes at certain times to His servants, the prophets, and that is what brought peace to me.

I started jumping up and down and woke my companion, shouting, "Yes, yes! You are right, Elder Jack! Heavenly Father and Jesus Christ appeared to the boy Joseph! This is the Lord's Church!"

A peace gradually enveloped my thoughts. The discouragement, sadness, and devastation I had felt earlier that evening were lifted. I felt a sense of quiet contentment enfolding me. I felt warm inside. This warmth continued to spread throughout my body. All I could think was how tender and sweet this feeling was, of knowing that my answer to my question lay in what happened in 1820. The Church of Jesus Christ of Latter-day Saints is led through revelation. While I did not know why certain things happened, I knew for a certainty that Heavenly Father reveals His will through prophets.

DEFINING MOMENT

This whole fiasco with the professor served as a defining moment for me and as preparation for what lay ahead. Interestingly, this discussion happened just over seven years after Zimbabwe's independence from the white minority as a British colony, so the issue of race and prejudice was the order of the day. It is humbling to think that although the prohibition was in place, Church leaders still battled with the issue for decades.

It is interesting that when one is having great spiritual growth and life-changing experiences, such as baptism, ordination to the priesthood, temple endowment, or missionary work, the adversary quietly sneaks in as a test of strength. After Moses had a great experience with the appearance of God, he was confronted by Satan. Satan demanded that Moses should worship him. Moses successfully rebuked Satan to leave him alone (see Moses 1:6–8, 12–14). The prophet Joseph Smith had a similar experience. Joseph Smith was determined that the only way he could know the answers to his questions was to ask God. In his attempt to do so, he was at first overcome by Satan's powers. With persistence and focus on his purpose, he conquered. The heavens were opened, with God's plan to offer salvation to all the world's people (see Joseph Smith—History 1:11–12, 13–17).

While the subject of the priesthood prohibition for those of African descent came to me while I was having great spiritual growth and life-changing experiences on my mission, I was not the only one. At least three others who have served or are serving in leadership in the Church had similar experiences while they were on their missions.

For Khumbulani D. Mdletshe, who joined the Church in KwaMashu Township, Durban, South Africa, the subject of a prohibition on the priesthood for those of Black African descent came while he was serving a mission in the England London Mission. Khumbulani has since served in different Church callings, including counselor in the stake presidency, Area Seventy, and mission president. Unlike me (I had not had an opportunity to participate in seminary before my mission), Khumbulani went on his mission five years after his baptism, having graduated from seminary. During door-to-door knocking in Brixton with his companion, Khumbulani learned for the first time about the prohibition on the priesthood for those of Black African descent. A tall Black man who opened the door accused Khumbulani of being a Black man who belonged to a racist Church. When Elder Mdletshe inquired why he would call the Church he loved racist, the man responded, "Mormons do not give the priesthood to Black people, because they believe that they are cursed." When the man discovered that Elder Mdletshe did not know anything about the priesthood prohibition, he explained what he understood to be the reasons the Church had denied the priesthood to Blacks. The man began expounding the scriptures, discussing the curse that Blacks had supposedly inherited from Cain and Ham with this utterly dumbfounded missionary.

This was enough to have this great young missionary pack his bags and return home. Khumbulani relates his experience: "After stewing over this for some time, I eventually decided that if what I had been told is true, I had no business representing a racist Church. I had been raised in a very racist country, and now, it appeared, I was a member of a racist Church." Khumbulani relates that by the time he decided to reach out to his mission president, he had already decided that he was going home. When he called his mission president, President Ed J. Pinegar, he invited Khumbulani to come to the mission office. While he was sitting in President Pinegar's office, he rehearsed what he had learned from the man during door-to-door knocking, and how because of that, he wanted to go home. After carefully listening to Khumbulani, President Pinegar confirmed that it was true that Black people had once been denied the priesthood by the Church. He said that no one knows the reasons. He then told this young missionary that what he knew was that all worthy men could now be ordained to the priesthood. With this honest, brief explanation from his mission president, Khumbulani decided to stay on his mission. This served as the defining moment in his life. As he relates, "That decision was life changing. The answer I received from my mission president that day has sustained [me] for more than three decades. I will ever be grateful to that man of God for his inspired words that day."

All the nonsensical theory about politics of the day and racism is meaningless to me. We need to view these men who have been and who are prophets, seers, and revelators in this dispensation of times from the perspective of Joseph Smith, who declared, "I understand my mission and business. God Almighty is my shield; and what can man do if God is my friend? I shall not be sacrificed until my time comes; then I shall be offered freely."[1] In the few years I have been able to be around these men, in my experience, they have no motive other than the worth of a soul. Being among them, I have felt the love of the Lord Jesus Christ through them. Their lives have been dedicated to serving the Lord, in ensuring that His children worldwide, regardless of nationality, race, color, or status, find peace and joy and prepare for the Lord's Second Coming. Brigham Young, who was a prophet in 1852, "publicly announced that men of black African descent could no longer be ordained to the priesthood." Subsequently, "Church leaders and members advanced many theories to explain the priesthood and temple restrictions. None of these explanations is accepted today as the official doctrine of the Church."[2] A loving Father in Heaven, who sees the big picture, seeing what I was becoming, reached out to me through my companion Francis Jack after our discussion with the professor and helped me to know through His Spirit that all was well. This was even before the Gospel Topics essays, which now provide explanations and answers to those earnestly seeking to know the truth about this subject.

In my recent discussion with Khumbulani, he added that his mission president asked him, "Since you have a testimony of the restored gospel, are you willing to walk away from it?" Khumbulani then said to me, "Of course, I did not want to walk away. I stayed. My testimony of the restored gospel continues to grow. These unanswered questions of the past continued to play a second fiddle."

The second person who also had this encounter with the prohibition on the priesthood for those of Black African descent was Elder Clement M. Matswagothata, an Area Seventy serving in the Third Quorum of the Seventy. Elder Matswagothata lives in Gaborone, Botswana. While Elder Matswagothata was serving in the South Africa Cape Town Mission, he came across a man who accused him of being used by the Church. Clement relates his experience as follows:

> We were knocking on doors on a cold winter's night in Cape Town, in a terrible rainstorm. Finally, a family let us in, and as we walked into the house the father dropped his head and told me how disappointed he was in me for letting the Church "use me" in such a way after all they had done to Blacks. I didn't know what he was talking about, and on enquiring further he took us through to his study, where he pulled out all kinds of books on Blacks and [prohibition on] the priesthood. I was shocked, since I had never heard

anything about the issue of race and the priesthood until that very hour.

As Clement left this home with his companion, he asked that they go and see the mission president right away. He related his experience to his mission president, who asked whether Elder Matswagothata was able to bear his testimony to this man. When he responded that he did not, his wise mission president asked him to return and bear his testimony of the Restoration of the gospel. With his companion's encouragement, they returned. This became a defining moment for this young missionary. He shared his experience:

> We drove back, and with tears in my eyes I testified to him of the power of the priesthood. Standing there on a cold winter's night, I received a sure knowledge of the priesthood and the Lord's timing on the matter. Since that night, I have had a solid conviction and a great sense of peace about the inspired process through which the priesthood was restored, and it has been one of the topics I have taught with power and authority.

As I heard the experiences of Khumbulani and Clement, I felt that the 1978 revelation to have all "worthy male members of the Church ordained to the priesthood without regard for race or color" was far more wide reaching through uplifting and inspiring than the prohibition on priesthood (Official Declaration 2).

The third person is Elder Idyo Raymond Egbo, Area

Seventy, who is in the Third Quorum of the Seventy. Elder Egbo lives in Nigeria. He narrated his experience as follows:

> I first became aware of the significance of the restoration of the priesthood to all races while serving as a full-time missionary in Lagos, Nigeria. My companion and I had been teaching the landlord of our apartment. He was excited about our message. However, our meetings ended after a cold reception from his wife on a follow-up appointment. She demanded we immediately stop teaching her husband. In her words, "Your church is made up of racists." We were ordered out of their home and told never to return. Her parting words were "go ask your church why Blacks are rejected from the priesthood." We found out later she had lived in Salt Lake City in the 1970s.

Even recognizing all the pain and confusion caused by the prohibition on the priesthood, Raymond was able to find peace and hope in the 1978 revelation on priesthood. He said that the priesthood restoration has increased his faith and the faith of his family, as they have seen how the priesthood has been a blessing in their lives.

GRATITUDE FOR THE PRESENT

Many of those from the continent of Africa that I have had the opportunity to interact with share the same feelings. They express gratitude for the gospel in their lives now, notwithstanding the range of feelings they might have about what happened in the past. As I share a few of those accounts here, my invitation is that you will feel their gratitude for the restored gospel and be inspired by their zeal to take the lessons of the past and move on with faith and determination. Indeed, "The past is to be learned from but not lived in. We look back to claim the embers from glowing experiences but not the ashes."[3] In essence, most leaders and members of Black African descent have relied on their testimonies of the restored gospel to come to understand and find peace about the revelation of the priesthood in 1978.

Elder Sibongiseni Ephraim Msane, Area Seventy in the Third Quorum of the Seventy, and his dear wife, Sister Nomthandazo S. Msane, first met the missionaries in Rotterdam, Netherlands. Elder and Sister Msane live in Johannesburg, South Africa. They were taught, felt the truthfulness of the restored gospel through the Holy Ghost, and were baptized. A few months after baptism, while Sister Nomthandazo Msane was visiting with a certain lady sharing the gospel, she learned about the priesthood prohibition. The lady told her that since she was Black, she could not join The Church of Jesus Christ of Latter-day Saints and related the history of Blacks and the priesthood. Sister Msane responded to her by saying that even so, she was a better person than before she joined the Church. As time went on, though, the former priesthood and temple restriction bothered her. She eventually asked her husband if he was aware of this. Elder Msane had not been aware of this piece of history. He related his experience:

> Though I thought it was strange and racist that such a thing would have happened, somehow it did not bother me much. We reminded each other of our testimonies. Somehow this kept us going and active in the Church until we were blessed with a better understanding of the Lord's restored gospel and His ways.

Here we can see the wise decision from Elder and Sister Msane to hold on to their testimonies. Holding on to what we have and remaining true to what we know is the key to our success in life.

William Coleman is currently serving as mission leader with his dear wife, Sister Philomina Coleman. President and Sister Coleman are serving in the Zimbabwe Bulawayo Mission. The couple is from Cape Coast, Ghana, in West Africa. They are both returned missionaries. President Coleman found out about the priesthood prohibition when he was already a member. Although this discovery disturbed him for a while, he kept it to himself. He said that the pain and concern he had was replaced by peace when one day he read, "These twelve Jesus sent forth, and commanded them, saying, Go not into the way of the Gentiles, and into any city of the Samaritans enter ye not: But go rather to the lost sheep of the house of Israel. And as ye go, preach, saying, The kingdom of heaven is at hand. Heal the sick, cleanse the lepers, raise the dead, cast out devils: freely ye have received, freely give" (Mathew 10:5–8). He said that he had an impression that if the Savior Himself had commanded His Twelve to go only to His lost sheep of the house of Israel, and then after His Resurrection asked them to go to all nations, who was William Coleman to accuse His servants of being racist or being unfair? He added, "All the pain, worry, and shaking of faith vanished and were replaced by peace, joy, and firm faith in Jesus Christ and His servants both past and present."

Elder Justice N. Otuonye, Area Seventy, serves in the Third Quorum of the Seventy. He is from Aba, Nigeria, in West Africa. He attributes his success in the Church to his parents: "My greatest joy, which has brought so much peace to my family and me, is to have been born of goodly parents who brought me to the knowledge of the truth through The Church of Jesus Christ of Latter-day Saints at a very tender age." Justice relates that when he was baptized at the age of eight, he was told that the most important thing was the priesthood authority to perform baptism and the laying on of hands for the gift of the Holy Ghost. The opportunity of growing through Primary and youth classes with great teachers and leaders helped shape his life.

When he learned about the prohibition on the priesthood for those of Black African descent, he had already experienced peace and joy as a priesthood holder. Justice observed, "Instead of dwelling on the questions like, 'Why did it take a longer period before the priesthood was given to those of Black African descent?' I strived to be worthy of it, acting in faith, following the established principles, and always giving thanks to God who gave the revelation in 1978, through the prophet and the Quorum of the Twelve Apostles, finding us worthy to hold His power."

I have a friend I have known for many years, since we were district presidents in the 1990s and later stake presidents in our different countries. He was a district and stake president in Nairobi, Kenya, and I was a district and stake president in Harare, Zimbabwe. Later, we sat as General Authorities in the Conference Center, being the only Black Africans for a few years. Elder Joseph W. Sitati, released with emeritus status now, during his ministry came to the same conclusion that he could increase his faith better by focusing on the future.

During his address at the Black, White, and Mormon conference on Friday, October 9, 2015, at the University of Utah, he said that while most members are aware of the reality of the past, their preference is to move forward, "and [they] have found individual answers in the restored gospel of the plan of happiness that gives them understanding and peace regarding the unfolding events of the gathering Saints in these last days." It is time for Africa. The continent now has over 700,000 members and is growing in leaps and bounds. Elder Sitati also observed, "Those [members] who have found answers choose to look forward to the future with faith and assurance that all things are before the Eternal Father, that His justice is to all men and that His redeeming love and mercy are extended to all who turn to Him with full purpose of heart." The central theme in these experiences is that with a sure knowledge of what happened in 1820, and a firm testimony of the Restoration of the gospel, nothing else matters as much. Are there lessons drawn from these experiences?

LESSONS FROM AFRICA IN FOLLOWING PROPHETIC COUNSEL

Yes, there are lessons. The lessons are that God works and reveals His will through prophets, seers, and revelators. While most of us joined the Church after the 1978 revelation on the priesthood, we are inspired by the early Black members who "continued to join the Church through baptism and receiving the gift of the Holy Ghost,"[4] despite not being able to receive the priesthood and temple blessings. Their faith and confidence in the Lord's prophets catalyze a strengthening of faith for generations to come.

These early Black members undoubtedly knew that a prophet is a teacher. His role is to teach his people true doctrine and prepare them for salvation and exaltation. They knew that the Lord gives commandments to His children through prophets.

A family friend who was in a class at BYU–Hawaii in the early 1990s shared that the class was going very well and a lot of the men in the class were excited to hold the priesthood. He said that as the class progressed and neared the end, one of the longtime members who was listening intently interjected and brought up the subject of Blacks and the priesthood. He inquired whether anyone was aware that the priesthood was withheld from Blacks until 1978. He continued to say that this was because the

Blacks were cursed and that the curse was only lifted in 1978.

Joel B. Chibota is currently serving as mission leader with his wife, Rose Chibota, in the Alabama Birmingham Mission. Joel was in that class at BYU–Hawaii. He said of the experience, "I must admit that the discussion took a turn that none of us expected. Hearing that was so painful, and testimonies were shaken, including mine."

Joel said that he quickly realized that the Lord had brought him here to His Church for a reason and that the Spirit had already borne witness to him that the Church was true. At that moment, he reaffirmed a resolution he had made before—that he would never let anyone or anything derail his testimony. With that determination, he lifted his head and looked into the faces of his fellow students. They looked shocked and devastated. Everyone looked at him, the only Black man in the room, with sympathy and sadness. Joel stood up and bore a firm testimony of the restored gospel of Jesus Christ and encouraged everyone to remain strong and faithful. Because the Church is true, nothing else matters.

Joel said that it was not easy to keep everyone motivated after this fiasco. Others started having doubts about the Church, including those who were generational members. "Sadly, some did fall away from the Church, but many remained active," he said. Joel completed his education at BYU–Hawaii and returned home to Zimbabwe, where he married Rose (Gondwe) Chibota. Later, during the Zimbabwe economic meltdown, Joel and Rose moved to Salt Lake City to seek further education and opportunities.

Ernest Sibanda was the first Black person to become a member of The Church of Jesus Christ of Latter-day Saints in Rhodesia (now Zimbabwe). At the time, Rhodesia was part of the South African Mission, and Brother Sibanda's baptism in Rhodesia preceded the 1978 revelation on the priesthood. He is one of those I mentioned earlier, whose faith and confidence in the Lord's prophets would catalyze a strengthening of faith for generations to come.

In February 1998, during President Gordon B. Hinckley's visit to Harare, Zimbabwe, while I was serving as a district president, we asked Ernest Sibanda and his dear wife, Priscilla, to sit on the front row next to Zimbabwe's first Black missionary, Peter Chaya, and his wife, Gladys, for this historical meeting held in our country with the President of the Church.

One day, Brother Sibanda had taught a junior Sunday School class, and, unaware of what might be the reaction of the children, he brought up the subject of the prohibition on the priesthood for those of Black African descent. Rose Chibota, who lived in Zimbabwe at the time and was in the Sunday School class, explained that when he did so, "There was a uniform gasp from the youth as we heard about how Blacks had not been allowed to hold the priesthood until 1978!" She said, "A part of me wanted to leave; another part wanted answers." Rose Chibota said that the day she learned about the priesthood restriction was a very hard day for her. She wasn't sure what to do. She had a lot of emotions. Her first emotions were disappointment, anger, and some feelings of betrayal. Rose felt that she had been lied to because she hadn't been told about this before her baptism. She was confused, and it took some time to process it.

Zimbabwe had just won its war of independence from the white minority, and so most Zimbabweans during this period in the early 1980s had a lot of tender feelings. Rose spoke to her friend Gillian about this discovery. Rose and Gillian chose to stay in the Church because they had strong testimonies of the restored gospel of Jesus Christ. Rose said that some of her fellow youth never came back to Church after that experience. Rose concluded by saying, "Over the years, I have held on to my testimony—it is what keeps me going. I chose to forgive the past and leave it in the hands of the Lord." What a blessing it is when we follow and act upon the impressions we receive rather than being "tossed to and fro, and carried about with every wind of doctrine, by the sleight of men, and cunning craftiness, whereby they lie in wait to deceive!" (Ephesians 4:14). As easy as it was for the children of Israel to look at the serpent and live, so it is with us today, to listen to the Lord's prophets and find peace and joy (see Numbers 21:8–9).

Those who left their missions or left the Church missed the opportunity to serve within it, to have joy as "fellowcitizens with the saints, and of the household of God" (Ephesians 2:19). I surely hope that all will eventually return to the fold. Consider the tender loving question from President M. Russell Ballard: "To whom shall we go?" President Ballard was referencing the Savior's Twelve

Apostles, who were asked by the Lord whether they would also leave since the disciples "went back, and walked no more with him" (John 6:66). President Ballard taught, "As these disciples left, Jesus turned to the Twelve and asked, 'Will ye also go away?' Peter responded: 'Lord, to whom shall we go?'"[5] President Ballard asks us to consider where we will turn if we turn away from the Church of Jesus Christ when our faith is tested.

Albert Mutariswa is my spiritual mentor. I mentioned him in my book *Beyond the Shade of the Mango Tree* as my bishop who taught me the principle and the blessings associated with tithing. Albert and his wife, Melion, recently returned from the Nigeria Enugu Mission, where they served as mission leaders. The couple joined the Church in October 1996, in the Mufakose Ward, Harare Zimbabwe Stake. Albert relates that shortly after he was baptized, he was asked a question by one of the distractors on why he had decided to join a racist church that considered people of African descent as inferior. He of course had not been aware of the priesthood prohibition. He quietly decided to research. Through his research and seeking enlightenment from the Holy Ghost through prayer, he felt at peace. Albert relates his experience as follows:

> My faith has grown tremendously because of the knowledge that I have acquired as I researched on this matter. I have also come to understand that it is more important to look into the future and the promised blessings that have been preserved for the faithful members, rather than

impede our personal growth because of events that happened in the past.

Albert and others' experiences, as well as faithful members across the African continent who were impacted by the prohibition on the priesthood for those of Black African descent, have to a large extent strengthened my faith. I am very grateful and inspired by their faith and testimony of what happened in 1820, and in the Restoration of the gospel, with the prophets, seers, and revelators at the helm of this work.

The world will be inspired and blessed by the lessons drawn here from Africa, of anchoring one's testimony on the doctrine and following and sustaining the prophets, no matter what the situation might be.

Throughout the ages, there has always been a price to pay for one's belief. We must withstand the adversary and find peace and joy, which comes through following the prophets, who point us to the Lord Jesus Christ.

As you prayerfully read the accounts of these African leaders and members, open your heart and be prepared to act on the impressions you will receive. As you do, you will find solutions to the challenges you currently face. For me, the invitation from the Lord to "look unto [Him] in every thought; doubt not, fear not" (D&C 6:36) and to heed His voice through the voices of His servants was impressed on my mind as I learned how these African leaders and members found peace and joy regarding the prohibition on the priesthood for those of African descent and the 1978 revelation on priesthood.

ONE-ON-ONE WITH PRESIDENT MONSON

On August 21, 2016, during President Thomas S. Monson's birthday reception in the boardroom of the Church Administration Building, I was filled with indescribable joy when President Monson spoke to me about his experience leading to the 1978 revelation on the priesthood.

On President Monson's 89th birthday, the General Authorities serving at Church Headquarters, along with staff members and others, were invited to a reception. This was my very first time attending a birthday reception in the United States of America. I must have gotten there earlier than most people, including President Monson. The receptions I was accustomed to were associated with lots of food. No wonder my eyes focused on the large table in the middle of the room. There were very beautiful decorations and lots of different snacks and fruits.

Noticing that those who came into the room would help themselves to a small plate of selected snacks, I joined them and enjoyed the delicious food. I thought that at some time, President Monson would come into the room so that we could sing "Happy Birthday" to him. It wasn't until Elder Joseph W. Sitati came in and started chatting with me that I realized that President Monson was already in the room. My mind and focus had been on the large table with eats, and I hadn't paid attention to what was happening around me. I learned from Joseph that most General Authorities who were coming in would go and shake President Monson's hand, pick up a few refreshments, and leave the room.

I was surprised to see that the room was almost empty, and looking at my watch, I realized that I had spent over an hour in the room, standing, eating, and chatting, without paying much attention. I immediately walked toward where President Monson was sitting. I stopped when I realized that Sister Harriet Uchtdorf was chatting with him and waited for my turn. When Sister Uchtdorf was finished, she walked to me and started chatting with me. She inquired about my wife, Naume, and the children. Sister Uchtdorf must have sensed my lack of concentration, as my mind was drawn to President Monson, especially realizing that I was the last person in the room, and I did not want to keep him waiting. I could even see from the corner of my eye that he was looking at me intently. Sister Uchtdorf graciously wished me all the best and left.

As I leaned over to greet President Monson, he reached out with both his hands, gently touched my shoulder, and brought me down so that he could look into my eyes. He then narrated to me the events leading to the 1978 revelation that every faithful, worthy man in the Church may receive the holy priesthood. He said to me, "I was there, and felt that it was time." He continued, "We all knew and felt it was time." I learned a lot about the process of revelation. Most of what he said was just for me. It is too sacred to share.

This one-on-one tutoring from President Monson on this subject left me with an overwhelming feeling of reverence and admiration for the role of prophets, seers, and revelators. The only other person in the room was President Monson's daughter, Sister Ann M. Dibb, who waited patiently. I felt the Spirit enlightening and edifying. Indeed, I felt indescribable joy!

Since that first evening in Bulawayo, Zimbabwe, as a young missionary at the professor's home, I have come to understand and find peace about the revelation on the priesthood in June 1978. I am convinced that any earnest-seeking person will receive answers and guidance from the Lord, as I and many of my African brothers and sisters have. If you have a firm testimony of what happened in 1820 and trust in the Savior, He will provide the peace that you seek.

"The rod of iron to which the faithful travelers were holding fast took them 'through the mist of darkness.' Not around, not over, not underneath. The route was *through*. The path to the tree of life did not bypass the pain. It required you to place your trust in God that you could make it *through* the pain. God assures us that even our afflictions can bear good fruit, as the Savior declared in a stunning promise: 'All things shall work together for your good, if ye walk uprightly' (D&C 90:24)."

–TRACY Y. BROWNING

HOPE FOR A BETTER WORLD

◇

TRACY Y. BROWNING

Sister Tracy Y. Browning was sustained as Second Counselor in the Primary General Presidency for The Church of Jesus Christ of Latter-day Saints on April 2, 2022. At the time of her call, she was serving on the Relief Society General Advisory Council. She has also served as a ward and stake Relief Society presidency counselor, as a Relief Society and Sunday School teacher, and in the Young Women organization. Sister Browning studied at St. John's University. She has worked in financial services for fifteen years and is now employed in the Church's Publishing Services Department. Sister Browning has also volunteered with various community and civic organizations. Sister Browning was born in New Rochelle, New York, in the United States. She grew up in Jamaica in the West Indies, and in New Jersey and New York. She married Brady Browning, and they are the parents of two children.

TURBULENCE

If I close my eyes and let my mind take me backward a little way, I can almost place myself tangibly in the moment. On a weekday, not dissimilar to any other, I was sitting comfortably in a cozy airplane seat, heading home, when it happened. The moment when I left the familiar cursoriness of takeoffs and landings, which I'd become accustomed to with air travel, and found myself displaced with building uneasiness as the plane ascended.

I've never been a nervous traveler. On the contrary, I generally find the journeying exciting. I love traveling to new places, knowing that my exploration will be long reflected upon—fond memories of experiences gained, potentially expanding myself in new ways and allowing my travels to add context to a world shared with others. I now realize that up until that day I had taken a few things for granted along the way. For instance, I'd never really given much thought to the airplane itself. I'd never considered the time it takes to build a machine to do the seemingly impossible, in defiance of gravity, and allow us to fly. Or the needed precision and years of engineering to come up with designs for each and every part of a plane's infrastructure. The testing, the retesting, the learning, the adjusting. I haven't spent a lot of time considering the skill, experience, and education of the pilot and copilots—the things they understand but that I couldn't even if I were to examine the collection of buttons and dials they employ to navigate the flight. Or the air traffic control tower and their managing the flow and traffic of innumerable aircrafts. Guiding pilots during those takeoffs and landings. And all the monitoring that happens as I sit comfortably in a cozy seat high up in the air.

Nor do I expend a lot of energy imagining turbulence. I suppose I have a generalized sense that I could encounter it. But, if I'm being honest, it's always somehow unexpected when it happens. It's an unwelcome surprise that, depending on the degree, aggressively punctuates an otherwise temperate experience. And I've come to recognize my natural habit is to view storm clouds as less vexing when I'm standing on the ground versus when I'm making a climb to higher elevation. From the ground, those clouds can suggest an obstacle earmarked for some future date because of how much more surrounding scenery there is to admire at the moment. I suspect it's an avoidance tactic that might come from isolating and misreading the 34th verse of Matthew chapter 6, which says, "Take therefore no thought for the morrow," when the 33rd verse teaches us how to acquire tools of righteousness that are meant to prepare us for all our tomorrows. So, when I was suddenly overcome with growing anxiety as our plane became enclosed in a thick, heavy, darkened mist, I couldn't have known just how instructive this singular occurrence would be on my preparedness for future challenges.

GOD IS FAITHFUL

It started with a feeling of claustrophobia. I was in a small plane. The kind where you can see the pilots from your seat. No steel door with security latches to separate you from the cockpit. Only a piece of black fabric suspended on a rod. And while that curtain remained drawn, there was a monitor in the wall in front of me that gave me a broad view of what they were seeing out of their windscreen—which was just more thick mist. It was then, as I stared at the monitor and turned my head left and right to look out of both passenger windows, that the feeling of being trapped by the oppressive mist took hold. With my vision obscured, and a tangible sensitivity to being separated from anything familiar or comforting, I could feel the weight of my surroundings. You couldn't convince me that the plane's ventilation system wouldn't very shortly be overcome by the outside air and I'd soon be breathing it in and having my lungs filled with the overwhelming fog. I sat imagining myself choking on it. I felt consumed by it, and in that state my trust started to crumble.

I tried to uphold some visible decorum, because after all, I wasn't the sole passenger on this flight. As I took quick glances around, I immediately recognized that everyone appeared to be calm. Some were quietly reading or dozing off into serene slumber. Even *I* was showing no outward reflection of the inward turmoil that I was experiencing. I felt compelled to "hold it together," to not create additional discomfort for the other passengers. But truthfully, a small acknowledgment, a knowing glance, could have eased the feeling of isolation of the experience. And for all I know, each of us seated on that plane that day could have been similarly masking our worries from each other. Coping in our own ways. Desiring a little bit of comfort, but not quite knowing how to give it under those circumstances—just as I was. So there I sat—feeling quite alone in my worries. Worries about the stability of the aircraft and the ability of the pilots to navigate through the thick of it. Surely, *they* must be as worried as I was, because I knew that they too could see nothing but the mist. The monitor and the windows were there, laying bare the reality of our circumstances. And here we were, climbing deeper and deeper into the hollowness. Moreover, I was filled with worry about how much longer I could endure the ascent. What was likely a few minutes felt like an eternity—an endlessness that was adding to the tightness in my chest.

Gratefully, I've developed a few responsive behaviors—especially when I'm in distress—that come from years of practiced experience. One of my favorite verses of scripture in the Book of Mormon is Jacob 3:1, which reads, "Look unto God with firmness of mind, and pray unto him with exceeding faith, and he will console you in your afflictions." So, to repel the feelings that had taken hold of me, I immediately began to offer a silent and fervent prayer for peace and relief. Praying to our Father in Heaven has always been what grounds me when I feel most untethered. I know He hears me because we've been in conversation for years. Our communications are deep and varied. Sometimes I reach out for counsel. Sometimes when I need clarity. Other times to share frustrations, or joys. Or at times just to sit in a particular quiet that I can only find when I choose to seek His presence. But I always express gratitude because I've come to recognize His dependable nearness to me when the storm clouds appear in my life. He has always offered an immovable support to catch hold of when the unexpected wind begins to blow all around me.

I know He hears me because just when I think I can't take any more, when I've reached the end of my ends, He endeavors to show me that "God is faithful," and that even in my suffering He will "make a way to escape" (1 Corinthians 10:13). And sometimes the escape is not just *liberation* from the moment's oppressive feelings.

Sometimes it's also a *lesson* that is an investment in my discipleship.

And I knew He heard me on that day because when we finally surfaced from the depths of the mist, I beheld the most glorious horizon. The sky was wonderfully blue. The sun shone luminously ahead of us—more incandescent than blindingly brilliant. For a few moments I sat with my eyes transfixed as we flew smoothly toward that clear expanse of sky. Eventually, our plane made a soft bend to the left, and then through my seat's window I felt the warmth of the sunlight, gentle and sweet against my cheek. I closed my wet eyes and swallowed the lump forming in my throat as my silent prayer reshaped to phrases of gratitude. I was happy, and I was on the other side. And my hands were fixed firmly to my Father's dependable support.

On that day, not dissimilar to any other, our faithful Father made Himself known to me in my silent and fevered pleading for liberation, and He did so with a profound metaphoric lesson—about the journey, the mist, the plane, about His immovable support, and about the horizon. And about how I can take all those lessons and apply them to other challenging circumstances in which I may find myself—other times when I might find myself suddenly struggling through the mist and fighting to not have it consume me.

STUMBLING BLOCKS

What I *can't* recall with any great specificity is the date or time I learned about The Church of Jesus Christ of Latter-day Saints having placed priesthood and temple restrictions for people of Black African descent prior to 1978. I joined the Church at sixteen, in the early nineties, and my instruction about the restored gospel of Jesus Christ from the missionaries and other Church members did not include anything about that part of the Church's history. Now, I don't believe anyone was intentionally trying to keep information from me or deceive me in any way. I think it's an uncomfortable part of the Church's history, which, frankly, I sense most people would rather not talk about, so they don't—unless they feel it's absolutely necessary. Like when asked a direct question. And even then, it's a difficult conversation to have, because we all desperately want a neat and tidy explanation. And too often we actually attempt to give one. Generally well-intentioned, but at times fumbling our way through to make it make sense, only to end up coming across as defensive. Or at other times, in an attempt to minimize pain and hurt, we forget to learn how to sit in the discomfort caused by the priesthood and temple restriction, demonstrating our understanding that no man-made explanation can alleviate the pain of it and have it emerge as tidy. This would be another place to start; a helpful step is to learn to simply acknowledge the hurt, and then try to point others to our Savior as the only truly stabilizing source on which to lean, with speculative reasons being so messy.

I suppose that the prevailing thought in the minds of many may be that since the restriction no longer presents a barrier for Black people to receive and participate in the fullness of the gospel—including all the ordinances and covenants of the gospel—then why place a stumbling block on someone's covenant path? A stumbling block is a circumstance that causes difficulty or hesitation. And truthfully, I understand this perspective to a large extent, given that I don't believe that the restriction's historical reality should stop any person (Black or otherwise) from joining Christ's Church, fellowshipping within His flock, and enjoying His covenant relationship. But don't misunderstand; I don't encourage keeping this information from each other. I wholeheartedly trust in the Spirit of God to overcome any concern and guide our Father's children to bind ourselves to Jesus Christ through the ordinances of His gospel found only in His Church. Our individual journey to those sacred ceremonies is unique, and each will come with unique feelings and experiences that may be a personal wrestle we bring before God. A yearning for Him to provide the Balm of Gilead to our pleas for peace. We don't have to mistakenly put ourselves in place of the miracles that the Spirit brings, believing that our silence on uncomfortable topics will somehow soothe a potential wound. God promises that "[He] will not to leave [us] comfortless," but assuredly "[He] will come to [us]" (John 14:18).

President Russell M. Nelson has taught that "on every continent and across the isles of the sea, faithful people are being gathered into The Church of Jesus Christ of Latter-day Saints. Differences in culture, language, gender, race, and nationality fade into insignificance as the faithful enter the covenant path and come unto our beloved Redeemer."[1] His guidance underscores our need to prioritize our Savior and our desire to covenant with Him as our primary objective. Other things that we may not have in common become subordinate to that end. But in our attempts to help gather God's children to His gospel and His Church, we need to be careful that our efforts innocently meant to assist others in navigating challenging topics don't themselves become stumbling blocks of our making (see Romans 14:13).

President Ezra Taft Benson, President of the Church from 1985 to 1994, gave an incredible message on "the great stumbling block to Zion"—Zion being representative of a people who are pure in heart. President Benson explained that pride is that stumbling block, and that it "is essentially competitive in nature." He taught that it pits "our will against God's . . . in the spirit of 'my will and not thine be done.'"[2] This competitive spirit robs us of the blessings that God offers in the present, as well as any ability to contextualize those gifts in the future, based on our obedience to His will. But as I've been able to have the advantage of inspecting the fruits of my obedience, I've learned that where God tells you that you belong, allow no man—including your own natural man—to convince you otherwise. Go where He tells you and leave it to Him to resolve the limited understanding of others, as well as your own in the present. His will always counsels us to follow God and then wait upon Him.

President Benson went on to further teach that we put ourselves in danger of not accepting the authority of God when we pit our "perceptions of truth against God's great knowledge," wishing God to agree with us rather than being "interested in changing [our] opinions to agree with

God's."³ In effect, allowing ourselves to create neat and tidy narratives around the present-day echoes of the experiences that were lived firsthand by our ancestors and predecessors, interjecting our own personal experiences that may inadvertently give shape to a retelling of that history. Occasionally communicating defensiveness, we tell an incomplete story in an attempt to make that history fit cleanly into modern-day, secular patterns whose roots lie in our existence in a fallen world. Both are limiting and offer no sustainable healing.

Speaking now to the latter of those two positions, I tend to believe that much of the world's history has shaped the experience for God's children of color, particularly God's Black children, as a life that has many unfortunate moments to be endured rather than purely enjoyed. As a result, many Black people approach the uncomfortable truths about our place in history, or our place in shared institutions, with a touch of expecting bad news. It's the dark cloud off in the distance that's earmarked for some future discomfort. But theoretically we're standing on the ground in the secular world, so we are inclined to try to find a way around the storm, looking about for alternate routes that circumvent ominous sky. The objective being a path forward without the turbulence that threatens to infringe on our present trajectory or into our future. As a diaspora people, we've had enough historical experience with the commotion of dark clouds. They create confusion like a lesson not quite learned and doomed to be repeated. We're all too familiar with the sound of that unpleasant echo, following closely behind us as we're trying to get out of the tunnel. The material world is strewn with stumbling blocks that Black people navigate almost daily, from everyday mundane tasks to more serious, life-threatening circumstances.

Speaking specifically on the need for racial harmony in America, President Nelson, in unity with three of his friends from the NAACP, Derrick Johnson, Leon Russell, and the Reverend Amos C. Brown, asserted that "the wheels of justice should move fairly for all. Jesus of Nazareth came that we might have life and have it 'more abundantly.' We should follow His example and seek for an abundant life for all God's children."[4] This desire for abundant life is a foundational aspiration that we all share, regardless of our backgrounds. But to me, one of the saddest realities is that Black people are very rarely surprised when we encounter obstruction on the way toward our abundancy of life. We may be outraged, we may be wearied—but, as a people, we're infrequently *surprised* by it. The fallen world can at times be a battle to try to not lose our balance. Consequently, we're eager to search for refuge from a world built of sand and clay. And I think for most of us, this is a hope we have in church. In a community of faith. A hope for sanctuary in a *spiritual* world. A hope for tools that help us navigate our way when aspects of these worlds, at times, collide.

My spiritual world, as a new convert, was filled to the brim with loving and lovely Church members who taught me gospel truths and bore powerful testimonies of Jesus Christ and His love for all God's children. But there were times when people outside of the Church would make attempts to pit those testimonies against their understanding of Church history. Or even times when, sadly, members of the Church would be thoughtless and careless with their words and actions that did not demonstrate consistent honoring of my identity as a child of God, and as their sister in Christ. On the lightest end of my experiences, I would be chided for joining a "white" church, even though I was fortunate in that my Church family reflected the global nature of the gospel, as well as the wonderful diversity of the New York City community that I lived in. Many of my leaders and friends were certainly white, but many were also Filipino, Polynesian, Latino, Korean, or Caribbean. They taught me that "all are alike unto God" (2 Nephi 26:33) and that the "worth of [my soul] is great in the sight of God" (D&C 18:10). That "there is no gift greater than the gift of salvation" (D&C 6:13) and that God offers freely (see 2 Nephi 2:4). They taught me that I could have all our Heavenly Father and our Savior Jesus Christ have (see D&C 132:19–20). And because of their witness and instruction, my life expanded through the gospel of Jesus Christ. The doctrine of Christ brought excitement, vibrancy, and meaning to everything. And moreover, *every gospel truth* I was taught was then confirmed and reaffirmed, many times, by the Holy Spirit that is present in my life.

On the heavier end of the spectrum, people would share what seemed like sound bites about the priesthood and temple restrictions—snippets of information that didn't feel like they were meant to be helpful, but rather to counter my personal conversion experience with skepticism and dismissal. At times I have struggled through Sunday meetings where ideas, attitudes, and teachings about race and/or the priesthood and temple restrictions, long abandoned by the Church and its leaders, were shared. But truthfully, these latter ordeals were the most personally challenging for me, because I hadn't yet developed a reservoir of spiritual experience in finding peace through our Savior when I was facing the seemingly inconsolable. So, I experienced a collision that I now recognize was the other occasion where I was metaphorically sitting in a comfortable seat, high in the air and homeward bound, in my spiritual sanctuary, when an "exceedingly great mist" arose to enshroud me (1 Nephi 8:23). It was threatening to crumble my trust, pitting my perceptions against the omniscience of God. I felt as if the weight of it might crush my chest or cause me to choke. I was left searching for something tangible to catch hold of and struggling not to lose my way. To not wander off and be lost in the thick of it. But that collision, ultimately, allowed me to deeply "know that all things work together for good to them that love God, to them who are the called according to his purpose" (Romans 8:28).

THE TREE OF LIFE

Some of the first things that came to my mind after my harrowing plane ride were some immediate parallels to Lehi's depiction of his vision of the tree of life as described in 1 Nephi in the Book of Mormon. This chapter and its adjacency to the experience I had on the airplane have helped me put into context my growth after crossing through the heavy emotions and struggles that came with the uncomfortable historical reality of the priesthood and temple restrictions.

In Lehi's account, the ancient prophet describes various journeys and trials of people getting to the tree of life, which is representative of the love of God and His giving of our Savior Jesus Christ to us for our salvation. Lehi, like our Savior, stands beckoning all in his family to come forward and offers the fruit of the tree, which represents the blessings of the Savior's Atonement, culminating with everlasting life (see 1 Nephi 11:21–22; John 3:16). The vision describes the trek that people take in their effort to reach the tree and partake of the fruit that is described as "desirable above all other fruit" and is "most sweet" with a promise to "make one happy" (1 Nephi 8:10–12). This vision is shared very early in the Book of Mormon, which in later years I've come to appreciate and look upon as a timely tool to help us examine the various efforts of the people in the ancient Americas and their dealings with God, as well as our own personal lifelong endeavors to get and stay on the straight and narrow path that leads to the tree of life. I now recognize myself in Lehi's vision as one of the many faithful who are earnestly pressing forward, and I have a renewed appreciation for what that experience of advancing could have entailed.

As I've pondered a few verses of chapter 8, I've gained some useful insight that helps me prepare for my present and future journeying home:

1. There is power in our choice to "obtain the path" and press forward.

In verses 21 and 22 we read:

> And I saw numberless concourses of people, many of whom were pressing forward, that they might obtain the path which led unto the tree. . . . And it came to pass that they did come forth and commence in the path which led to the tree.

As I study these two verses, the word *obtain* consistently strikes me. The scripture *could* have simply said "get on" or "access" the path, or some other variation. But it doesn't. It says "obtain," and as I've studied the etymology of that word, I've learned the visceral strength of it. Its Latin root means "to take hold of" and to "hold fast." These descriptors provide more visually striking imagery about the faithful traveler's decision to get to the tree of life. They add more urgency, importance, and determination to the choice to walk toward Jesus Christ and take hold of His offering of eternal life. Our strong regard for the gift of agency that we have, which allows us to choose God, provides fertile ground in our life for the gospel to be deeply planted and take root. It is the conditioning that makes "obtaining" possible. The people depicted in Lehi's vision were able to find and start on the path because they decided that's what they wanted for their life. And the level of urgency, importance, and determination associated with that choice seems to me to subtly foreshadow what is to come next—an innate sense that their choice to walk the path that leads to the tree requires strong care and far less casualness. We read in verse 23 the following:

> And it came to pass that there arose a mist of darkness; yea, even an exceedingly great mist of darkness, insomuch that they who had commenced in the path did lose their way, that they wandered off and were lost.

After the travelers made a powerful choice to focus on reaching the Savior and took steps to enter the path, they found themselves in the midst of turbulence. And even worse, they lost their way. President Thomas S. Monson taught, "We who chose the Savior's plan knew that we would be embarking on a precarious, difficult journey. . . . Although in our journey we will encounter forks and turnings in the road, we simply cannot afford the luxury of a detour from which we may never return."[5] Our choice points us and focuses us on our Savior Jesus Christ, but it does not exempt us from any turbulence we encounter along the journey. Our righteous choice then becomes amplified with the assistance of additional tools that help us *remain* on the right path.

2. Catch hold of the iron rod and hold fast to it.

Verse 30 helps us to understand the differences in experiences between the faithful travelers on the path who were inevitably lost to the thick mist versus those who were able to remain on the path. We read the following from that passage:

> They came and caught hold of the end of the rod of iron; and they did press their way forward, continually holding fast to the rod of iron, until they came forth and fell down and partook of the fruit of the tree.

Here we learn that there were many who recognized that they had been provided something stable, tangible, and available for them to catch hold of when their vision became obscured by the mist—when they must surely have felt panicked as they moved from one experience along their journey to another. And that stable and immovable support is identified as "the rod of iron," or the word of God. The scriptures promise that those who hearken to it—and listen and act accordingly—would "never perish," or be overcome by temptations designed to blind them and lead them off the path (1 Nephi 15:23–24). Verse 30 again gives a sense of what this experience must have been like for them, because the language that is used to describe the behavior of the people is so visually striking. They are said to be "continually holding fast." My mind's eye sees people who are trying to direct all their energy, their faith, and their focus to hanging on to the promises and assurances found in the word of God for their survival. Holding fast to it so that they are not consumed by the anguish caused by the mist. How much then do we need to become intimately familiar with the word of God so that if—or when—the time comes, our reflex will be to grab on to the rod in the depths of the pain and sorrow of the mist enshrouding us?

3. Go THROUGH the mist.

The next part of verse 24 that I found particularly instructive was that the rod of iron to which the faithful travelers were holding fast took them "through the mist of darkness." Not around, not over, not underneath. The route was *through*. The path to the tree of life did not bypass the pain. It required you to place your trust in God that you could make it *through* the pain. God assures us that even our afflictions can bear good fruit, as the Savior declared in a stunning promise: "All things shall work together for your good, if ye walk uprightly" (D&C 90:24). Going through the mist when considering the priesthood and temple restrictions might look like examining the limited historical record against the light and lens of modern-day truth found in abundance in the scriptures, along with the words of modern-day prophets and apostles. That journey through the mist may be shorter for some and longer for others. Our individual experiences and feelings as we consider how to press forward through that mist may be different. I've found appreciation and similarities to my own experience as I've read of President Dallin H. Oaks's process of prayerfully studying the speculative reasons for the priesthood and temple restrictions. He said, "I studied the reasons then being given and could not feel confirmation of the truth of any of them."[6]

When I similarly studied Church materials and historical documents that surrounded the priesthood and temple restrictions, I did not feel the Spirit confirm truth about what was detailed. In fact, what would consistently be placed in my mind and then confirmed, reconfirmed, and reaffirmed, were the gospel truths that were taught to me in my early years of discipleship. Namely, that "all are alike unto God" (2 Nephi 26:33) and that the "worth of [my soul] is great in the sight of God" (D&C 18:10). That "there is no gift greater than the gift of salvation" (D&C 6:13), and that God offers it freely (see 2 Nephi 2:4). That I could have all our Heavenly Father and our Savior Jesus Christ have (see D&C 132:19–20).

The study to invite peace and some level of understanding was difficult. The content was painful. And it took me *through* the mist. But I held on to the word that God was planting deeply in the fertile ground of my faith and of my life lived by continually choosing God and being obedient to His will. Because I trusted the scriptures that taught, "He that keepeth his commandments receiveth truth and light," and "light and truth forsake that evil one" (D&C 93:28, 37).

It did not escape me that as I went through my study, that included holding in my heart a pleading prayer to the Lord for an answer to the question, *Why did this happen?* His reply was always to repeat the truths I had been taught earlier and then to guide me to understand one other gospel truth. When we come to the Lord in earnest, with hearts open to Him, He will answer each of us in the way that is best for our individual needs. And that reiterated response He was giving was what was needful or expedient for me (see D&C 88:64). I think this could be similar to the learning President Oaks described: "As part of my prayerful study, I learned that, in general, the Lord rarely gives reasons for the commandments and directions He gives to His servants."⁷ My effort now was to hold fast to and ponder on the truths found in God's reply while safeguarding myself from any additional stumbling blocks that could place my desire for more specificity in opposition to all of God's great knowledge—effectively, putting myself at risk of letting go of the rod that I know is there and that is meant to be the lifeline that saves me from wandering off into the mist and becoming lost. We are asked to trust Him to pilot us home. At times He sits behind a thin curtain, just out of view. And at His disposal are all the tools of an omniscient God, which I would only be feigning comprehension of if I actually had the opportunity to get a glimpse. He knows so much more than I. My "whys" next to His will feel fragile. But His word is unbreakable.

4. Partake of the fruit. It's "sweet above all that is sweet" (Alma 32:42).

The scriptures don't tell us how long the travelers spent pressing forward through the mist. And if it was anything like my plane ride, the actual time of it might be inconsequential compared to the feeling of experiencing it. But what we do know is that they "did press their way forward, continually *holding fast* to the rod of iron, until they came forth and fell down and partook of the fruit of the tree" (1 Nephi 8:30; emphasis added). Their diligence in not letting go of God's word as they passed through the discomfort was rewarded by them reaching the tree and partaking of the fruit. I again reflect on that moment that I burst through the overwhelming fog of that plane ride. How I was filled with such relief and gratitude to be on the other side of it. To be greeted by the warmth of a luminous sun. To feel its sweet caress on my cheek. It was the realization of the good fruit that the Savior promises when I try my best to keep my promises to Him. There will come a point, in all the emotional capital expended to go through our challenges, even on something like coming to a full view of the priesthood and temple restrictions, where we are promised that there is a way to emerge and come forward into the warmth of the sun. Be believing in the promise. And then when you're there, finally feeling like you can breathe again, and finally having your vision restored—like stepping out of a darkened room and into the light—savor all the sweetness that only Jesus Christ can offer. Rejoice in it. Weep over it. And thank God for it.

5. Be not ashamed.

One of my great hopes for the Second Coming of our Savior Jesus Christ is an end to the adversarial intrusion of the material world into the spiritual one. It never fails that in the world in which we live, airplanes must eventually land on the ground, placing us back among secular distractions that make it easy for the memory of our significant spiritual experiences to fade or be exposed to the derision of others. And so it was for some of the faithful travelers in Lehi's vision who made it to the tree of life and partook of the fruit. In verses 26 through 28, we read:

> And I also cast my eyes round about, and beheld, on the other side of the river of water, a great and spacious building; and it stood as it were in

the air, high above the earth. And it was filled with people, both old and young, both male and female; and their manner of dress was exceedingly fine; and they were in the attitude of mocking and pointing their fingers towards those who had come at and were partaking of the fruit. And after they had tasted of the fruit they were ashamed, because of those that were scoffing at them; and they fell away into forbidden paths and were lost.

As is true in the present, so it was in ancient times, that not everyone will understand, respect, or value the choices you make to come to know God. And taking your eyes off the Savior in order to entertain their judgments and speculations about your walk toward Jesus Christ ultimately leaves you exposed to drifting away from your hard-fought testimony. For me, as discussed earlier, that represented the many who were either trying to shame me for joining such a "white" church or whose "sound bites" on the Church's priesthood and temple restrictions were meant only to dismiss my earnest testimony about the experience I had walking to the tree of life. The secular world will always have a "great and spacious building" filled with people who will be your friend only if you join them in the scoffing of faith. But common sense tells me that a building suspended in the air, with no solid foundation, sounds like questionable craftsmanship and is doomed to come crashing down at some point. Nothing significant exists there. No greater truth, no brighter light, no lasting joy that we should trade for the tree and the fruit. Be not ashamed; you're choosing the better path.

JESUS CHRIST OVERCAME THE WORLD, AND SO CAN WE

God told me when I was sixteen years old that The Church of Jesus Christ of Latter-day Saints was His Church. That the Book of Mormon was His word. That prophets and apostles still lived and guided His work. That I was to gather myself with His people, in the water and in the temple, and make covenants with Him. He told me that I belonged; that I was His. That I was purchased with the blood of our Savior Jesus Christ. That my inheritance was eternal life with God the Father, and God the Son. And He told me that the melanin in my skin, or the skin of my children, or the skin of my ancestors, would never change these truths. Not even an uncomfortable part of the Church's history can change it. The gospel of Jesus Christ is not racist, and He stands at the head of His Church. And I know that whenever His children are in peril of being lost to the mist, the rod of iron is available to provide clarity and to keep us pressing forward toward the tree of life.

I'm not ashamed to be a member of Christ's Church. I could never cast my eyes downward in shame after every miracle, every personal revelation, after every communication I've had from the source of all truth, whose name is "Wonderful, Counsellor, The mighty God, The everlasting Father, The Prince of Peace" (Isaiah 9:6). The world may not ever understand how a Black woman could joyfully join herself with this community of believers of Christ, even when I bear my soul through spiritual testimony. What *I* struggle to understand is why these same people never seem to have questions about my life in the secular world, with its own expansive history of sorrow and pain toward my people. I guess somehow the daily decisions I make to navigate or circumvent the land mines found in that world make sense to them, but somehow the reality of God assuring me that He will always support me in His sanctuary does not. And in His sanctuary, we are promised that "whoso believeth in God might with surety hope for a better world, yea, even a place at the right hand of God, which hope cometh of faith, maketh an anchor to the souls of men, which would make them sure and steadfast, always abounding in good works, being led to glorify God" (Ether 12:4).

I rejoice in the restored gospel of Jesus Christ that has the audacity to speak boldly that God would save His children. That sings to us, "Fear not, little children, for you are mine, and I have overcome the world . . . ; and none of them that my Father hath given me shall be lost" (D&C 50:41–42). I sit in awe at this Church that taught this most hopeful truth as a whisper inside of the howling of the prevailing teachings that exclaimed there to be only one heaven and one hell. I weep with joy at the kindness and mercy of our God who provides us with liberation and escape from our deepest sorrows. Who invites us to hold fast to Him, feel how solid He is, and to stand on His firm foundation. To be brought to gaze upon the effulgence of His horizon, and then to partake of His most desirable fruit. He knows you must be hungry. He understands that the climb can be harrowing for you. But look down and see where your hand is. It's still firmly holding fast to His.

NOTES

DIRECTED BY HIS LIGHT
CAROL LAWRENCE-COSTLEY

1. See David A. Bednar, "Patterns of Light" (video), ChurchofJesusChrist.org.
2. Russell M. Nelson, "Let God Prevail," *Ensign*, November 2020.

THE REVELATION THAT CHANGED THE WORLD
AHMAD S. CORBITT

1. Because the dream is so sacred, it remains private to me and my family.
2. In this part of the mass, attendees shake hands and wish each other peace.
3. Doctrine and Covenants, Official Declaration 2.
4. I was not one of those truly valiant Black Latter-day Saints who joined the Church prior to the revelation. Seven of us were baptized in 1980. Dad followed in 1981, and the oldest child was baptized in 1994. The three youngest were baptized as they came of age.
5. Oddly enough, I don't remember the moment when I learned of the priesthood restriction. While I was writing this essay, I was told by a good friend that at the time of my baptism, I asked "a lot of tough questions" about the ban. While I am sure this is true, I don't remember it. My earliest memory of talking about the ban was when I was a full-time missionary teaching a Black man in St. Croix, U.S. Virgin Islands. He had served at Hill Air Force Base near Ogden, Utah, where he had heard several times about the restriction. He was incredulous that I, as a Black person, could be a Mormon. So while I don't specifically remember struggling with the ban, early on in my Church membership it became a challenge to help others overcome so they could experience the deeper and sweeter fruits of the restored gospel that lay beyond it.
6. It was about this time that I heard a talk that had a great impact on my life, "Another Testament of Jesus Christ," by President Dallin H. Oaks. Citing the teachings of President Ezra Taft Benson, President Oaks invited the Church to repent for not remembering the Book of Mormon and its essential feature of salvation through Jesus Christ. See *Ensign*, March 1994.
7. Joseph Smith, in *Teachings of Presidents of the Church: Joseph Smith* (2007), 49.

NOTES

8. President James E. Faust taught: "We do not lose our identity in becoming members of this church. We become heirs to the kingdom of God, having joined the body of Christ and spiritually set aside some of our personal differences to unite in a greater spiritual cause. We say to all who have joined the Church, keep all that is noble, good, and uplifting in your culture and personal identity. However, under the authority and power of the keys of the priesthood, all differences yield as we seek to become heirs to the kingdom of God, unite in following those who have the keys of the priesthood, and seek the divinity within us. All are welcomed and appreciated. But there is only one celestial kingdom of God. Our real strength is not so much in our diversity but in our spiritual and doctrinal unity. For instance, the baptismal prayer and baptism by immersion in water are the same all over the world. The sacramental prayers are the same everywhere. We sing the same hymns in praise to God in every country" ("Heirs to the Kingdom of God," *Ensign*, May 1995).
9. Note this observation by President Henry B. Eyring: "Everything Alma and his people [at the Waters of Mormon] were inspired to do was pointed at helping people choose to have their hearts changed through the Atonement of Jesus Christ. That is the only way God can grant the blessing of being of one heart" ("Our Hearts Knit as One," *Ensign*, November 2008; emphasis added). President Russell M. Nelson taught: "Differences in cultural background, language, gender, and facial features fade into insignificance as members lose themselves in service to their beloved Savior. Paul's declaration is being fulfilled: 'As many of you as have been baptized into Christ have put on Christ. There is neither Jew nor Greek, there is neither bond nor free, there is neither male nor female: for ye are all one in Christ Jesus'" ("Teach Us Tolerance and Love," *Ensign*, May 1994). President Howard W. Hunter taught: "I suggest that you place the highest priority on your membership in the Church of Jesus Christ. Measure whatever anyone else asks you to do, whether it be from your family, loved ones, your cultural heritage, or traditions you have inherited—measure everything against the teachings of the Savior. Where you find a variance from those teachings, set that matter aside and do not pursue it. It will not bring you happiness" (in Richard G. Scott, "Removing Barriers to Happiness," *Ensign*, May 1998). We must be careful not to focus more on lesser, cultural matters, such as racial or ethnic identity, than on eternal identity and salvation through Christ. Those who focus more on cultural identity than spiritual identity invert the two great commandments, putting their identities in relation to God below their identities in relation to culture (see Matthew 22:36–40).
10. Henry B. Eyring, "Our Hearts Knit as One," *Ensign*, November 2008.
11. Jeffrey R. Holland, "Remember Lot's Wife" (Brigham Young University devotional January 13, 2009), speeches.byu.edu.
12. See Alma 5:15–17.
13. One effective way to respond is to help others understand relevant history, as the Church's essay titled "Race and the Priesthood" does (see https://www.ChurchofJesusChrist.org/study/manual/gospel-topics-essays/race-and-the-priesthood). Such an approach may include an

explanation that other churches and religions have also imposed restrictions based on race. I believe that in taking this approach, we should avoid addressing these issues in ways that tear down other religions. Also, we should be careful, in these days of growing secularism and atheism, that we don't diminish faith in general.

14. Dallin H. Oaks, "Be One" celebration remarks, June 1, 2018.
15. Brigham Young, in *Teachings of Presidents of the Church: Brigham Young* (1997), 87; see also Doctrine and Covenants 76:94.
16. As the people in the Savior's early Church apostatized more and more in their views and actions, the Lord no longer filled vacancies when members of the Quorum of the Twelve died. The absence of Apostles led to even more fracturing and splintering in the ancient Church. These fractures, and the schisms and reformations of subsequent centuries, demonstrate the need for Apostles to keep the Church unified.
17. So, while the Lord was "well pleased" with His newly restored "true and living church" (D&C 1:30), it seems obvious to me that He did not consider it complete when it was organized in 1830—it still needed to be built up. It needed to "become," just as God's children need to "become." On the principle of individuals "becoming," see Dallin H. Oaks, "The Challenge to Become," *Ensign*, November 2000.
18. Bruce R. McConkie, "All Are Alike unto God" (address delivered to religious educators, August 18, 1978), 3, speeches.byu.edu. In this message, Elder McConkie also said: "We get our truth and our light line upon line and precept upon precept. We have now had added a new flood of intelligence and light on this particular subject, and it erases all the darkness and all the views and all the thoughts of the past. They don't matter anymore."
19. These brethren said they "pleaded long and earnestly in behalf of these, our faithful brethren, spending many hours in the Upper Room of the Temple supplicating the Lord" (Doctrine and Covenants, Official Declaration 2). Before the Lord revealed that the blessings of the priesthood were to be extended to all people, Church leaders were supportive of faithful Black members of the Church who were waiting to receive those blessings. President Boyd K. Packer recalled a meeting he and others had during that period with the Genesis Group, an organization of African American Latter-day Saints: "We shook hands with all of them there, our brothers and sisters in that Genesis Group. They need our help, they need our prayers and our blessings and they need our attention. They really need our attention" (in Lucile C. Tate, *Boyd K. Packer: A Watchman on the Tower* [1995], 227).
20. "Now this prophet, small in physical stature but a spiritual giant, wrestled again, seeking and pleading in behalf of the faithful among all priesthood-denied people. Not only did he struggle, seek, and plead, but his brethren in the highest councils of the Church did so as well" (Lucile C. Tate, *Boyd K. Packer*, 225).
21. Heidi S. Swinton, *To the Rescue: The Biography of Thomas S. Monson* (2010), 393.
22. Gordon B. Hinckley, "Priesthood Restoration," *Ensign*, October 1988.

NOTES

23. Lucile C. Tate, *Boyd K. Packer*, 227.
24. Over the years, I have found that people's views of the priesthood revelation can often be described using two metaphors that make the same point. First, the priesthood revelation can be like a mirror in which people see what they bring to it. The second metaphor is the well-known half glass of water. Some, who can't seem to get beyond Church history and are thus unable to focus on what the Savior called "the weightier matters"—"judgment, mercy, and faith" (Matthew 23:23), or the work of salvation—see the revelation in "half-empty" terms. To them, so long as they are in this frame of mind, the revelation will always represent the negative thing it terminated. They might demand that some further step be taken because a ban once existed. Others see the glass half full, with the revelation on the priesthood as part of the process of filling it up. They understand the scriptures and the living prophets and recognize that the Lord is adding to and building up His kingdom. Because they depend on the Lord, rather than the philosophies and approaches of the world, to be their Shepherd, their cup runneth over (see Psalm 23:5).
25. See Doctrine and Covenants 88:73.
26. Throughout the history of the Church, inspired questions have led to revelation and greater spiritual power for individuals and the entire Church. In contrast, fault-finding, judgmental, and condemning questions, especially in criticism of the Lord's servants, have generally worked in the opposite direction. Many of the revelations in the Doctrine and Covenants and other revelations to the Church, including the revelation on the priesthood, resulted from inspired questions. No wonder so much time and effort is spent training our full-time missionaries to ask such questions. An entire section of *Preach My Gospel* is devoted to appropriate and inspired questions that invite the Spirit of God. We would all do well to learn the lessons the missionaries are taught in this regard: "Jesus Christ often asked questions to help people ponder and apply principles. . . . Learn to ask questions as prompted by the Spirit. The right type of question at the right time can greatly help those you teach to learn the gospel and feel the Spirit. Likewise, the wrong type of question or a question at the wrong time can interfere with their learning. Asking appropriate questions at the right time requires that you are in tune with the Spirit" (*Preach My Gospel: A Guide to Missionary Service* [2004], 183–84).
27. Some will not be satisfied with this type of analysis. Those who are conditioned to blame-thinking will find it difficult to engage in forward-thinking, even in the absence of all the facts. Yet forward-thinking with inspired questions is the type of perspective Jesus Christ urged His disciples to engage in, following His example. I believe He wants His modern-day followers to catch this same forward-looking vision.
28. The Lord often uses this pattern—creating something grand from something perceived as problematic, insufficient, or difficult—to capture the attention of His children and to show His power. This pattern is found throughout the scriptures. See, for example, Doctrine and Covenants 1:17–24 and Judges 7.

NOTES

29. Henry B. Eyring, "Our Hearts Knit as One," *Ensign*, November 2008.
30. "High on the Mountain Top," *Hymns* (1985), no. 5.
31. Henry B. Eyring, "Our Hearts Knit as One," *Ensign*, November 2008.
32. Ezra Taft Benson, *The Teachings of Ezra Taft Benson* (1988), 167.
33. Howard W. Hunter, in *Teachings of Presidents of the Church: Howard W. Hunter* (2015), 124; emphasis added.
34. Howard W. Hunter, "All Are Alike unto God," Brigham Young University devotional (February 4, 1979), speeches.byu.edu.
35. Statement of the First Presidency, February 15, 1978.
36. Russell M. Nelson, "Christ Is Risen; Faith in Him Will Move Mountains," *Liahona*, May 2021.
37. Dallin H. Oaks, "Racism and Other Challenges," Brigham Young University devotional (October 27, 2020), speeches.byu.edu.
38. Henry B. Eyring, "Our Hearts Knit as One," *Ensign*, November 2008.
39. Dieter F. Uchtdorf, "Heeding the Voice of the Prophets," *Liahona*, July 2008. President Uchtdorf also said: "Faith in Jesus Christ and a testimony of Him and His universal Atonement is not just a doctrine with great theological value. Such faith is a universal gift, glorious for all cultural regions of this earth, irrespective of race, color, language, nationality, or socioeconomic circumstance" ("Precious Fruits of the First Vision," *Liahona*, February 2009).
40. Russell M. Nelson, "Be One" celebration remarks, June 1, 2018.
41. Gospel Topics, "Race and the Priesthood," https://www.ChurchofJesus Christ.org/study/manual/gospel-topics-essays/race-and-the-priesthood.
42. Gordon B. Hinckley, "The Need for Greater Kindness," *Ensign*, May 2006.
43. Dallin H. Oaks, "Be One" celebration remarks, June 1, 2018; emphasis added.
44. Dallin H. Oaks, "Love Your Enemies," *Ensign*, November 2020; "Racism and Other Challenges," Brigham Young University devotional (October 27, 2020), speeches.byu.edu.
45. Russell M. Nelson, "Let God Prevail," *Ensign*, November 2020; emphasis added. See also 2 Nephi 26:33.
46. Russell M. Nelson, "Let God Prevail," *Ensign*, November 2020.
47. Henry B. Eyring, "That We May Be One," *Ensign*, May 1998. See also John 17:18–21.
48. Henry B. Eyring, "Our Hearts Knit as One," *Ensign*, November 2008.
49. Henry B. Eyring, "Our Hearts Knit as One," *Ensign*, November 2008. I believe God's children have an inherent spiritual desire for harmony and equality with their brothers and sisters of other races and ethnicities. This spiritual desire may be why racial and ethnic unity are, I believe, more widespread in these vital last days than they have been at any other time in the history of the world.
50. Please note that I am not suggesting that the Lord caused the priesthood ban so He could at some later time use it for His own purposes.
51. What about Church members and other faithful persons of African descent who lived and died during the priesthood ban? We have every reason to believe that the faithful Black people of African descent who died

during the former priesthood ban can receive the restored gospel's full blessings and dwell eternally in the celestial kingdom with their loving Heavenly Father. I feel the same about the faithful who participated in the founding of the United States, or the Enlightenment periods preceding it, or the Middle Ages, or as Gentiles at the time of Jesus's personal ministry, or at any other time when the priesthood or the gospel has not been available to a particular group. For God has revealed, "All who have died without a knowledge of this gospel, who would have received it if they had been permitted to tarry, shall be heirs of the celestial kingdom of God; also all that shall die henceforth without a knowledge of it, who would have received it with all their hearts, shall be heirs of that kingdom; for I, the Lord, will judge all men according to their works, according to the desire of their hearts" (D&C 137:7–9). Similarly, the Prophet Joseph Smith taught: "The Great Parent of the universe looks upon the whole human family with a fatherly care and paternal regard; . . . and without any of those contracted feelings that influence the children of men. . . . He will judge them 'not according to what they have not, but according to what they have.' . . . He will award judgment or mercy to all nations according to their several deserts, their means of obtaining [light and truth], the laws by which they are governed, the facilities afforded them of obtaining correct information, and His inscrutable designs in relation to the human family" (*Teachings of Presidents of the Church: Joseph Smith* [2007], 39). It seems clear to me that our Father in Heaven has made provision to receive unto Himself His Black children who were unable to receive all the blessings of the gospel but who would have received them if there had been no priesthood restriction. This creates a significant opportunity for spiritual growth and energy on the part of Black Latter-day Saints and other members of the Church today—to perform temple work for deceased ancestors who have been waiting to receive the gospel's full blessings.

52. "The Family: A Proclamation to the World" *Ensign*, November 2010. Additionally, the First Presidency published the following statement in 1978, just months before the priesthood revelation: "Based upon ancient and modern revelation, The Church of Jesus Christ of Latter-day Saints gladly teaches and declares the Christian doctrine that all men and women are brothers and sisters, not only by blood relationship from common mortal progenitors but as literal spirit children of an Eternal Father" (quoted in Howard W. Hunter, "The Gospel—A Global Faith," *Ensign*, November 1991). President Russell M. Nelson has taught: "On every continent and across isles of the sea, the faithful are being gathered into The Church of Jesus Christ of Latter-day Saints. Differences in cultural background, language, gender, and facial features fade into insignificance as members lose themselves in service to their beloved Savior. Paul's declaration is being fulfilled: 'As many of you as have been baptized into Christ have put on Christ. There is neither Jew nor Greek, there is neither bond nor free, there is neither male nor female: for ye are all one in Christ Jesus'" ("Teach Us Tolerance and Love," *Ensign*, May 1994).

53. Russell M. Nelson, "Teach Us Tolerance and Love," *Ensign*, May 1994.

NOTES

President M. Russell Ballard taught this principle as follows: "Surely good neighbors should put forth every effort to understand each other and to be kind to one another regardless of religion, nationality, race, or culture. . . . I have been a member of this Church my entire life. I have been a full-time missionary, twice a bishop, a mission president, a Seventy, and now an Apostle. I have never taught—nor have I ever heard taught—a doctrine of exclusion. I have never heard the members of this Church urged to be anything but loving, kind, tolerant, and benevolent to our friends and neighbors of other faiths. The Lord expects a great deal from us. Parents, please teach your children and practice yourselves the principle of inclusion of others and not exclusion because of religious, political, or cultural differences" ("Doctrine of Inclusion," *Ensign*, November 2001). See also Henry B. Eyring, "A Priesthood Quorum," *Ensign*, November 2006.

54. See Ahmad S. Corbitt, "Activism vs. Discipleship: A Message for Chaplains of The Church of Jesus Christ of Latter-day Saints" (address to Church-endorsed chaplains, October 4, 2022), https://cdn.vox-cdn.com/uploads/chorus_asset/file/24159863/Brother_Corbitt_Chaplain_seminar.pdf.

HE WILL PROVIDE THE PEACE YOU SEEK
EDWARD DUBE

1. Joseph Smith, in *History of the Church*, 5:259.
2. Gospel Topics, "Race and the Priesthood," https://www.ChurchofJesusChrist.org/study/manual/gospel-topics-essays/race-and-the-priesthood.
3. Jeffrey R. Holland, "The Best Is Yet to Be," *Ensign*, January 2010.
4. Gospel Topics, "Race and the Priesthood," https://www.ChurchofJesusChrist.org/study/manual/gospel-topics-essays/race-and-the-priesthood.
5. M. Russell Ballard, "To Whom Shall We Go?," *Ensign*, November 2016.

HOPE FOR A BETTER WORLD
TRACY Y. BROWNING

1. Russell M. Nelson, "Be One" celebration remarks, June 1, 2018.
2. Ezra Taft Benson, "Beware of Pride," *Ensign*, May 1989.
3. Ezra Taft Benson, "Beware of Pride," *Ensign*, May 1989.
4. President Russell M. Nelson, "Locking arms for racial harmony in America," Medium.com, June 8, 2020.
5. Thomas S. Monson, "The Three Rs of Choice," *Ensign*, November 2010.
6. Dallin H. Oaks, "Be One" celebration remarks, June 1, 2018.
7. Dallin H. Oaks, "Be One" celebration remarks, June 1, 2018.